Y0-CBH-798

DAVID TARRANT'S

Canadian Gardens

DAVID TARRANT'S
Canadian Gardens

Whitecap Books
Vancouver / Toronto

Whitecap Books
Vancouver/Toronto

Edited by Liz Primeau and Rebecca Hines
Cover design by Warren Clark
Interior design and typesetting by Margaret Ng
Special thanks to Warren Clark
Cover photograph by Ryan McNair
Garden plan illustrations by Bonnie Summerfeldt Boisseau

Printed and bound in Canada by D.W. Friesen and Sons Ltd., Altona, Manitoba

Canadian Cataloguing in Publication Data

Tarrant, David.
David Tarrant's Canadian gardens

Includes bibliographical references and index.
ISBN 1-55110-193-9

1. Gardening—Canada. 2. Gardening—Canada—Pictorial works.
I. Title. II. Title: Canadian gardens.
SB451.36.C2T37 1994 635'0971 C94-910419-1

CONTENTS

Introduction

ardening in Canada is indeed a challenge, but keen gardeners find a way no matter where they live. This book is a testament to that.

I well remember that just before I moved to Canada in 1967, my mentor in the U.K., Frances Perry, tried to convince me to go to the U.S. instead. She said she knew of many good gardens there, but none in Canada. At the time she was principal of Norwood Hall Horticultural College, where I took my training and received a diploma in horticulture. Among other things, Mrs. Perry was the first woman member of the Royal Horticultural Society Council, an avid gardener, lecturer and garden writer. I am happy to say her first visit to Vancouver some six years later changed her mind. "If I were thirty years younger, I'd move here in a minute," she told me.

Over the past twenty-six years I have had the opportunity to garden in Ontario, high in the Rocky Mountains of Alberta, and in British Columbia, at the University of British Columbia's Botanical Garden, where I am education coordinator. The working atmosphere at the garden has allowed my career to flow over into the world of television: for ten years I was co-host, with Bob Switzer, of the CBC's nationally aired *The Canadian Gardener*, and for the past two years I have hosted it alone. The program has taken me to all the provinces and into the Yukon Territory, and I have been fortunate to visit countless gardens.

Gardeners are amazing people. They share a common thread no matter where they live. Traditionally, new gardeners plant according to the hardiness zone map, choosing plants the experts say are successful in their zone designation. But this usually doesn't last long. They soon realize that while the zone map has its place, there are many microclimates within it—and plants don't consult it in order to grow. The most challenging statement you can make to any gardener is, "Of course, you can't grow *that* here." It's like throwing down the gauntlet.

Another typical characteristic of dedicated gardeners is that they read all the latest books and magazines about gardening and attend as many lectures as they can, filling their heads with all the do's and don'ts of their avocation. Then, once in their own gardens, they do what they darn well please. And that's as it should be—the garden is one place you should be able to express yourself exactly as you want.

On the pages of this book you will be introduced to twenty completely different gardens across this vast country. Because of the way life is, two of them have changed hands—their owners have moved to new homes, where they are creating new gardens. The gardeners are individuals, too, each with his or her own approach to garden styles and to plants—including their names. To some a poppy may be a *Papaver orientale* or *Papaver rhoeas*, but to others it's just a poppy. The hard work of gardening is considered by some to be recreation, while to others it's therapy, removing them from the strains of the office, the fax machine and electronic mail. But all the gardeners possess two outstanding traits: enthusiasm and generosity. They've shared with us their secrets of success, from composting and mulching to the importance of good winter snow cover. I hope their experiences will inspire you to create a garden of your own.

Above: Lilium *'Casa Blanca' in full bloom.*

And so I want to express our thanks to all the gardeners featured in this book who were so willing to share their gardens with us. Special thanks also to my colleagues at the University of British Columbia's Botanical Garden, especially Bruce Macdonald, Judy Newton, Mary Nugent and Gerald Straley for their support and encouragement.

Last but not least, a big thank you to Liz Primeau for her help and careful editing of the text, and to Janet Champion for retyping the manuscript. And, of course, to Whitecap Books, to *Canadian Gardening* magazine and to the Canadian Broadcasting Corporation, for recognizing the importance of gardening in Canada.

DEDICATION

To Dorothy and George Crate, my aunt and uncle,
who introduced me to this great country and gave me my start here.

The English Garden

of Sharon Edey

Photographs by Bert Klassen

It's not by mistake that Sharon and Brian Edey's billowing garden just north of Bowmanville, Ontario, looks like it was transplanted from England. The garden overflows with masses of flowering plants spilling from generous beds, and the scent of roses and sweet williams is hypnotic on the evening air. "At our first house we created a park-like setting, with lots of lawn and shrubs," says Sharon. "We liked it fine, but then I went to England." She instantly fell for the unmanicured, cottage-style English gardens, their jolly mixtures of colourful plants tumbling over the edges of paths and into each other, filling the garden with colour for long periods of time. "I brought home a head full of ideas, and when we built this home nine years ago they started to come to life."

Above: *A rustic path leads through perennials to the cool woods beyond.*

Their house is a charming heritage-style structure of blue-painted clapboard with white gingerbread trim on a two-acre (.8-hectare) lot. As Sharon's ideas come to life, the garden beds keep growing, requiring a lot of maintenance. Sharon wouldn't refer to it as work, however. "We all spend a great deal of time puttering in the garden," she says of her family of four children. "Gardening is a family hobby, and was from the time they were small. If it weren't for Brian and the children, we couldn't have this garden."

For example, Michael dug the hole and made the cut-stone edging for the fish pond; Carolyn helps plant the two hundred spring bulbs they add to the garden each fall; Phillip does much of the garden maintenance, and Mark learned so much from working in the garden with his mom he's turned his knowledge into a summer job at a nearby garden centre.

Bonnie Summerfeldt Boisseau

Previous page: *Old-fashioned perennials, such as yellow loosestrife* (Lysimachia punctata) *and delphiniums, line the crazy-paving path.*

After nearly nine years, the Edeys' garden looks well established, but it required careful planning as well as a lot of work. The site is on a former gravel pit and several truckloads of topsoil were needed before anything would grow. Trying not to feel overwhelmed by the plans she had in mind, Sharon wisely grassed the lot the first year and put in a foundation planting of shrubs, trees and vines near the house. "The flower borders that spill out from them follow the curve of the front path and evolved naturally," she says. Over the years more beds have been added, one at a time, and like all gardens it continues to evolve.

The flagstone path curves gracefully from the front gate and leads to the porch, over which rambles silver lace vine (*Polygonum aubertii*). Native to western China and Tibet, where winters are cold, it's a hardy and attractive choice: its large, lacy panicles of blossoms show up well against the blue and white house. Along with it is a wisteria which will be lovely, once it blooms. Wisteria can take seven years or more to flower, but gardeners are a patient lot.

The long-established borders at the front of the house and the newer ones behind it are crammed with plants. "I tend to overplant," says Sharon. "It squeezes out the weeds, but the real reason I plant so closely is because I like a garden to look old and used." It's obvious that she also likes pink and a mixture of annuals and perennials, which achieves the full, long-lasting effect she wants. She combines pinks well: there are tall, pink annual cosmos (*Cosmos bipinnatus*), resident in all parts of the garden; various shades of pink daisies; the spectacular pink and mauve spider flower (*Cleome hasslerana*), which reaches a mature height of over three feet (one metre); and purple coneflower (*Echinacea purpurea*), its stiffly erect stems topped with large pink-mauve daisies centred with bronzy pincushions. The pinks are complemented by white shasta daisies (*Chrysanthemum* x *superbum*), lavenders, delphiniums, lupins, peonies and poppies. Wild purple Michaelmas daisies, a native plant seen in southern Ontario meadows in fall, have also been welcomed to the borders.

Below: *Red pelargoniums are a bright accent on Sharon's old-fashioned porch.*

The flagstone patio and weathered picket fence at the back were family projects a few years ago, and the patio is the location for summer meals. Between the stones creeping thymes have taken hold, offering pink blossoms in high summer and a pleasant aroma all season when trodden upon. Sweet white alyssum cushions out between the stones and into the nearby path, offering its fragrance in late summer and fall.

In spring the patio is surrounded by flowering bulbs, powder-blue forget-me-nots and deeper blue periwinkle. A nearby bed holds magnolia and rhododendron, underneath which white trilliums flower.

Past the backyard swimming

he corduroy paths that add so much to Sharon Edey's garden are easy to make if you live in the country and frequently have to thin out a woodlot. The trunks or stems of two- to three-year-old saplings are usually straight, and make a lovely base for an informal pathway.

First establish the location and width of the paths—two feet (sixty centimetres) is a minimum. Mark the path with stakes and strings, then remove about six inches (fifteen centimetres) of sod and top soil, incorporating it in flower beds or the compost heap. Lay a sand base, and define the edges of the path with long, straight saplings. Cut other saplings to fit the width of the path, and lay them side by side snugly together or, as the Edeys have done, with six-inch (fifteen-centimetre) gaps between them and embedded firmly in the soil so they aren't a hazard to unwary strollers. The crosspieces must be carefully cut so they sit firm and snug on the ground, wedging the side pieces in place.

For a woodland path, moss can be encouraged to fill in the spaces. In a drier sunny spot, use woolly thyme to interplant the gaps.

pool is the former vegetable garden. "I finally admitted it was flowers I enjoy growing," says Sharon. "Anyway, we live in the heart of market gardening country and can get fresh vegetables all season." So the vegetables were banished, leaving only a well-established asparagus patch and an area devoted to herbs. The rest of the space is taken up by flowers grown for drying and making up into gift arrangements—strawflowers (*Helichrysum bracteatum*) in many shades, *Statice sinuatum* in blue, pink and magenta,

Above: Spiraea arguta *'Aurea' and* Oenothera missouriensis *combine to make a bright summer scene.*

and larkspur (*Consolida regalis*), another favoured resident of old cottage gardens. Its spikes of blue, pink and white flowers closely resemble the perennial delphinium, which Sharon grows and dries for winter bouquets.

Beyond the pool and the dried-flower garden is a natural slope that can be seen from the house. At the top is a quiet little wooded area where thoughts can be gathered. Sharon has planted the slope with a multitude of flowering shrubs, daffodils and tulips that welcome the early spring.

They are followed by summer perennials. "The soil is very sandy here and dries out quickly, so we had to run an irrigation system through it for emergency watering," says Sharon. But many plants grow well here—yarrow (*Achillea millefolium*), peonies, lupins and rudbeckia, chrysanthemums and cosmos, which bloom well into the fall.

Every spring the Edeys buy a load of topsoil, which they store in a back part of the garden for using through the summer. A large truckload of mushroom compost is also brought in from a neighbourhood mushroom farm. "We use it immediately to top-dress existing plantings," says Sharon. "It's wonderful—odourless, and a good, crumbly mix." The abundance of maple leaves on the property is composted in fall, and what's left of the topsoil is used to hill up the roses and tender shrubs for winter.

Garden magazines are Sharon's favourite bedtime reading and she keeps a clipping file of ideas she likes. She also keeps a photographic record of her garden and takes snapshots of others she admires. "They come in handy when I'm deciding on changes," she says. Right after Christmas the seed catalogues are consulted and orders made up. The first seeds are sown indoors in February. When spring finally arrives the whole family helps in the garden, lifting and dividing large clumps of perennials, digging new areas, altering old ones. Sharon Edey says the mark of good gardeners is that they never leave anything alone.

Left: *A rocking chair on the porch is a perfect spot from which to contemplate the garden.*

Right: *Magnificent delphiniums catch the summer light.*

The Pacific Garden

of Vern & Joan McMurray

Photographs by Paul Bailey

erhaps it was impulsiveness that made Vern and Joan McMurray purchase their Victoria house more than twenty years ago, but there's nothing unplanned or haphazard about the garden that surrounds it. It all began when the McMurrays arrived too early for dinner one evening at their friends' home while on a visit to Victoria. They decided to drive around to pass the time, and turned down a small lane. A "for sale" sign in front of a wild property overlooking the sea caught their eye. The next day, they viewed the 1.7-acre (.7-hectare) property and rundown house with a real estate agent. On their way home to St. Albert, Alberta, they made a decision: the property would be theirs. Once home, Joan started to draw up plans for a renovated house and garden. And what plans they were: during the next two years, they drew up sixteen different sets of designs for the garden—and they hadn't even moved yet. Joan eventually settled into the refurbished house in 1978, and Vern commuted weekly until 1985, when he semi-retired. (He still returns to St. Albert occasionally to keep up with their small business.)

Above: *Hybrid tea rose 'Troika'.*

The well-planned garden has evolved into a multitiered setting for an extensive collection of rhododendrons, roses and herbs. Vern grew up in Surrey, England, where rhododendrons abound in the woods, while Joan, also from England, was surrounded by roses. Today they have over four hundred rhododendrons and dozens of roses. "All English gardeners love roses," Joan says. "Once the rhododendrons finish blooming, the roses take over."

Although their decision to purchase the property was quick, the McMurrays made no rash moves when deciding what to eliminate from

Bonnie Summerfeldt Boisseau

Previous page: *The rhododendron border is at its peak in early spring.*

Right: *A scarlet rhododendron and gold azalea contrast brilliantly.*

their overgrown property. Stately old Douglas firs (*Pseudotsuga menziesii*) and a magnificent pair of Garry oaks (*Quercus garryana*) with sinuous grey-green, lichen-covered trunks were spared when a long circular driveway went in. The oaks cast intricate patterns on the lawn, and provide welcome shade in the summer. Also saved were a lovely old apple tree and large, berry-laden English holly (*Ilex aquifolium*).

House renovations were adjusted to accommodate choice specimens. A gigantic camellia bush reached the eavestrough at the west end of the house. "Vern wanted to extend the house at this end, but I said he couldn't cut the camellia down. It was too big to move, so he built on to the other end of the house." Even an old arbutus stump was preserved, and now supports intertwining rose and clematis. Once the McMurrays had decided what they wanted to save, they turned their attention to new projects. Joan, the record-keeper, kept track of what plants were purchased and where each was planted, while Vern enlarged the garden, taking care to capitalize on its microclimates: frost in the upper part of the garden but none on the water side.

The first major planting was a cedar hedge on the west side of the property, for a necessary windbreak. It now backs a border of rhododendrons. Next they planted a magnificent sequoia (*Sequoiadendron giganteum* 'Pendulum') in the hope it would arch over the new driveway to welcome visitors to the garden. However, it had a mind of its own, and instead arches toward the west, away from the driveway.

Soon Vern and Joan were running out of level ground for their expanding collection of plants. Joan yearned for a formal herb garden, so Vern brought in ten yards of fill to create enough space near the western edge of the property. Under the high canopy of a tree, it's open to the

ne of the problems when growing rhododendrons on the Pacific coast of Canada is the weevil. Those snout-nosed little beetles are lethargic by day, but at night they can be observed with a flashlight, chewing neat little notches out of rhododendron leaves, giving each an etched design. Vern and Joan McMurray don't use chemical pesticides and they have tried all the homemade remedies for getting rid of these pests. One method is steel wool wrapped around each rhododendron trunk. Another tried-and-true method is tanglefoot, which is painted on the trunks: the beetles get stuck in it and can't make their way to the leaves. Both methods work well if the shrubs are single trunked, and as long as none of the branches grow out horizontally near the ground.

The McMurrays have finally found a product that works for them like a charm. It's a powder that contains nematodes, which attack the larvae stage of the weevil. The nematodes don't harm the foliage but work only in the ground—and only when the soil is moist and warm. Nematode products are a bit costly but, if mixed and used properly, one package will treat a thousand rhododendrons.

south, where light reflected from the sea helps the plants thrive. The beds, edged with cotton lavender (*Santolina chamaecyparissus*), germander (*Teucrium chamaedrys*) and dwarf boxwood (*Buxus microphylla*), overflow with culinary herbs and others Joan uses in potpourri.

At the edge of the herb garden the land slopes away toward the sea through a forest of wind-pruned Garry oaks. More of Vern's hard work is evident in the paths and steps leading to another level area, a circular enclosed garden room with chairs and a table for sipping afternoon tea; its inner walls are covered with ribbons Joan has won for her rhododendrons. Raised beds bordered with rocks are full of perennials, miniature roses and a *Clematis montana*, which has climbed one of the oaks to form an umbrella of pale pink blossoms each spring.

The McMurrays continued to extend their garden farther and farther from the house, into steeper and rockier areas of their property. Vern has

brought in some soil, but most of what's now there was scraped away from rocks and amended with oak-leaf compost. "We didn't want to bring in much new soil because weeds always come with it," Joan says. They continue to add oak-leaf compost annually to help keep the thin soil's nutrient level high.

Farther along the paths, in the dappled shade of the oaks, grow more rhododendrons. The McMurrays are involved in the local rhododendron society, which means they have added many unusual species to the hybrids they originally planted. Corsican mint (*Mentha requinii*) is planted among the paving stones, and its scent is released as visitors make their way to a dry stone retaining wall and a pond Vern built using rocks on the property. A recirculating pump helps a waterfall trickle down past the feet of two bronze cranes in the pond.

Vern's current project, in the wild area on the rocky cliffs near the ocean, involves removing vicious blackberries and mounds of moss. He's scraping more soil from the rocky outcrops for yet more new beds. Water is scarce in the summer, so Vern adds underground irrigation to each new bed as he goes along. It won't be long before this enthusiastic couple takes their garden right down to the shore.

Above: *Rhododendrons grow well in the cool shade of a Douglas fir.*

Right: *Vern's pool supplies the finishing touch to his terrace.*

The Family Garden

of Dwayne Eadie

Photographs by Brian Harder

ardening is a challenge no matter where you live, but when you add a couple of preschool children to the equation you have more than a challenge, you have an Everest to climb. Many budding gardeners postpone the idea until the children are past the swing set and sandbox age, or confine their own areas to perimeter perennial borders, leaving the lion's share of the space to the kids.

Not so Calgary's Dwayne Eadie: when his daughters were three and five, he designed a garden that integrated their play area and his flower beds with such flair that it will look good even after the kids are teenagers. To boot, the Eadies live in Calgary, where winters are long and gardens are at the mercy of the chinooks. In the dead of winter, warm air from the Pacific Ocean sometimes sweeps over the Rocky Mountains and flows down the eastern side into southern Alberta; temperatures can rise as much as seventy-seven degrees Fahrenheit (twenty-five degrees Celsius) in an hour. Humans, of course, bask in these momentary bursts of spring during a frigid winter, but the alternate freezing and thawing is extremely hard on plants, to say nothing of the dehydration.

Above: *Petunias and sweet peas provide brilliant summer colour.*

Dwayne Eadie, however, has learned to work with existing conditions. His garden is both pretty and practical, comprising the play areas, flower and vegetable beds, and a convenient patio where the whole family can cook, eat, lounge and in general enjoy the sunny Alberta summer.

The major colour is packed into a large, central raised bed that takes advantage of the gentle upward slope of the property and incorporates a horseshoe-shaped bike path made of crushed red shale that looks like an

Bonnie Summerfeldt Boisseau

***Previous page:** The children's swing and slide are integrated into the garden.*

expansive garden path. "Before I started to plan the garden I made a list of all the things it had to include, and important among them was the play space," says Dwayne. "But how? I watched the girls at play and realized they ran or biked in endless circles. So I decided on the bike path. It's also perfect for tag, foot races, hide-and-seek, and it allows *me* access to the flower beds."

At the top of the path the slope levels off; here is where the swing set and slide are located, partially hidden by shrubbery, as well as the "mechanics" of the garden: the compost bins, shed and vegetable garden.

Before Dwayne could plant in earnest he had to consider his garden soil, "a heavy alkaline clay." So while he was creating the path and digging the beds he incorporated well-rotted farmyard manure and spent mushroom manure. "I still like to add mushroom manure annually as a mulch. It's a great soil conditioner."

Colour in the centre bed is derived from a combination of perennials and annuals. Bright magenta gayfeather (*Liatris spicata*), a plant native to the central plains and prairies of North America, is an integral part of the garden and takes pride of place at the top of the bed. Mullein (*Verbascum thapsis*), a handsome plant with architectural interest that's been gaining in popularity in recent years, is also featured in the central bed. It forms a large basal rosette of downy silvery leaves up to eighteen inches (forty-five centimetres) long the first season, and the following year sends up three-foot-high (one-metre) flower stalks dotted to the top with sulphur-yellow blossoms. "The children love plants that grow above their heads," says Dwayne. Another favourite—this time Dwayne's—is the white *Campanula salicifolia*. "It's a tough grower," says Dwayne, "and it always flowers well no matter what the summer is like." Lady's mantle (*Alchemilla mollis*) tumbles over the front edge of the wooden retaining wall at the front of the bed and its lovely, soft green maple-shaped leaves sparkle with raindrops in a summer shower. Next to it grows the contrasting, linear-leaved perennial alyssum (*Alyssum saxatile*), which is covered early in the season with masses of minute frothy golden blossoms. Coral bells (*Heuchera sanguinea*) takes on a vivid hue in Calgary's clear summer air. Purple coneflower (*Echinacea purpurea*), another prairie native, contrasts with the white spiky flowers of obedient plant (*Physostegia virginiana*) (dubbed thus because the individual flowers massed up the stem can be gently moved into different positions). "It's a fascinating plant for children to play with," says Dwayne. Spiderwort (*Tradescantia* x *andersonii*) is another common but little-used plant that appears in this garden. It has wide, bright-green grass-like leaves and attractive, three-petalled bluish-purple flowers.

Below: *The children's cycle path surrounds Dwayne's mixed annual and perennial bed.*

More colour is provided by an old cottage-garden favourite, rose campion (*Lychnis coronaria*), which has downy silver leaves and strong erect stems topped with a multitude of maroon-red flowers. Annuals such as petunias and *Lavatera trimestris* with its big pink trumpet-shaped flowers bloom freely in the southern Alberta climate, seeming to try to pack a lifetime of colour in a few weeks of sun and warmth.

Shrubs and more perennials fill the beds on the outer edge of the bike path. Close inspection reveals some of the clever design techniques Dwayne has adopted. Through the centre of each bed he buried dividers made of heavy lumber. "They're the same as I used for the central raised bed," he says. "My idea was that they'd prevent the shrub roots from taking over the perennial area. But the children discovered them, and used them as a balance beam —they walked on them through the bed to observe the flowers and insects at close range." His garden, he says, has become a miniature nature classroom for his daughters. A network of stepping-stones through the borders

etting up the circular path for the children's bicycles was a simple task, says Dwayne Eadie, but he stresses that its width was important: there had to be room for at least two tricycles side by side. His path is three feet (one metre) wide. He marked the boundaries with string tied to bamboo canes pushed into the ground, then removed the top six inches (fifteen centimetres) of topsoil, adding it to the garden beds. He lined the path with a heavy-gauge construction-cloth liner and edged it with bricks (the depth of the path is about the width of a brick). The space was then filled with local red shale gravel, which is easy to rake. The gravel's terra cotta colour makes it easy to find after it's been inadvertently tossed onto the lawn or flower beds by skidding bicycle tires.

was deliberately placed with the children in mind, to encourage them to get as close to the plants as possible. They also prevent soil compaction and muddy shoes when Dwayne needs to carry out maintenance, such as weeding and pruning.

Dwayne's ability to pack many interesting plants into a small space also shows up in these borders. A couple of hardy *Potentilla fruticosa* add colour with masses of golden-yellow buttercup-like flowers all summer long, and there are roses—a real challenge in this area: a 'Hansa' rose from Dwayne's grandmother's garden, and an enormous *Rosa rubrifolia*, with its strong, metallic-looking, reddish-purple foliage and a succession of sweetly scented, single pink flowers throughout the summer. Below it is a fine spirea 'Anthony Waterer', a low-growing shrub covered with flat umbels of rose-coloured blossoms in summer. Not far from it grows the very hardy spirea 'Gold Flame', a commanding plant with glowing gold foliage in fall. For the children Dwayne has also planted many shrubs with edible fruit—Nanking cherry (*Prunus tomentosa*), for example, which has pretty white blossoms nearly an inch (two centimetres) across in spring, followed by an abundance of tasty fruit usually used for pies and jellies. There are also red currants. "Initially I thought the birds were getting all the fruit, but then realized the children were eating it," Dwayne says.

He feels that letting the children participate in the building of the garden gave them a sense of ownership and responsibility. "But you have to be prepared for thousands of questions," he says. "Kids never let go when they want an answer." He also suggests parents purchase child-sized gardening tools. "For the first couple of years, while we were making this garden, I was followed around by a shiny plastic kid's wheelbarrow loaded with the exact same materials I was hauling," he laughs. "The girls always wanted to know why there were bees in the garden, or spider webs that caught other insects. Just answering their questions taught them so much about the environment."

He admits to the occasional minor disaster. More than once a pathway miraculously appeared through a flower bed where none existed before. Of course, no one admitted responsibility. At other times annuals have disappeared only to appear like magic in a new spot. Gravel from the path frequently ends up in the flower beds. But these incidents are always quickly forgotten. "The positive effects of letting children take an active part in the garden will last through their lives and outweigh my minor annoyances," he says.

Dwayne also included in the garden design a raised wood deck at the kitchen side of the house. It has a shaded area for hot days, storage areas, seats, a dining area and a hammock. He and his wife spend many a warm summer evening on the deck after the children have gone to bed. Scented annuals such as sweet peas and petunias, which send out their sweet scent after the sun goes down, are planted nearby. Planter boxes overflow with geraniums, marigolds and dusty millers; scarlet runner beans and herbs grow near the house, ready for plucking. This truly is a garden that the whole family can enjoy. "When I was a kid I had to weed my family's garden," says Dwayne. "At the time I never thought it would have an impact on my later life. But it did. I'm carrying on the tradition with my children because I believe gardening awakens them to our environment."

Left: *The patio at the side of the house provides an outdoor living room for the whole family in summer.*

Below: *A prolific apple tree and mixed annual flowers, such as Shirley poppies* (Papaver rhoeas) *and catchfly* (Silene armeria), *grow in the children's own garden.*

The Japanese Garden

of Patrick Kelly

Photographs by David Ventrudo

hunder Bay seems an unlikely location for an extraordinary Oriental garden, especially one created by a law-enforcement officer who's never been to Japan. But as a child Patrick Kelly helped look after the Oriental garden of an elderly couple. Their pond and rock garden, and the way large rocks were placed for certain meaning, had a profound effect on him. Years later, a small book on Japanese gardens sent to him by his brother, a missionary in the East, convinced him that an Oriental garden was his heart's desire.

Patrick Kelly's present Japanese garden is not his first. "The first one—complete with a stream and a bridge, stone lanterns and a teahouse—was much smaller," says Patrick. I'd come home from work on the Thunder Bay police force and feel embraced by the serenity of it. It helped me keep my sanity."

Above: *A Chinese egg pot* tsukubai *with hand-crafted bamboo accessories nestles between junipers and hand-picked rocks.*

In 1976 he and his wife, Rosemary, moved to their new home in a subdivision. The lot, ninety by forty feet (26 by 11.2 metres) with four hundred feet (122 metres) of city parkland behind it that cannot be developed, was irresistible. "There was nothing here," says Patrick. "No trees, no stones, not even any grass. And no hydro or phone wires to clutter the view. It was waiting for me. Right away I had a picture in my mind of what I wanted, and we progressed one step at a time."

But these were difficult steps, requiring many hours of heavy work. Rosemary and Patrick worked together to bring in hundreds of stones and rocks, all carefully chosen in the wild, loosened with a crowbar, and carried by wheelbarrow to a trailer custom-built for transporting rocks. Perhaps the most beautiful rock in the garden is visible

Bonnie Summerfeldt Boisseau

***Previous page:** A waterfall cascading into a still pond brings serenity to an Ontario lakehead forest.*

as one enters: rectangular, shaped like a chaise lounge but a little larger, it represents a celestial ship bearing treasures from the heavens. A similar rock reposes in the Daisenin garden in Kyoto, but Patrick found this one in a nearby lake. On a subzero March day, Patrick and his brother-in-law, Walter Bahry, took a four-wheel-drive truck and a five-ton chain block and drove over the lake ice to the north shore, where the rock stood. They hooked it up, got it on the truck and hauled it back to the more easily accessible south shore, where they left it. In spring the celestial ship sank as the ice melted, and when the weather was suitable, Patrick backed his truck into the water and winched the rock onto it. "It stands where I placed it to this day," says Patrick, "and it looks as though it was always meant to be there."

Another rock-hauling story must be shared. The flat, black stepping-stones that lead to the bridge across the pond were spotted by Patrick in a local river on one of his rock-scouting missions. Collecting them would be a simple matter, he thought, and one day in mid-July, when the river was at its lowest, he and Rosemary drove out to get them. But they had not realized how steep the riverbank was, and after levering out the rocks with their trusty steel crowbar, they had to push them up the bank in the wheelbarrow. "The scene was like a Laurel and Hardy movie," laughs Patrick. "I was pushing the wheelbarrow up the bank, while Rosemary was behind pushing me, and collapsing with laughter."

But a visitor to the garden is not aware of the comic tales behind the gathering of the rocks, and sees only their serenity and permanence. Rocks lend a sense of character and age to a garden, and that's one reason the Japanese use them. In Patrick's garden they have the same effect, combined with the calm sounds of water and the visual appeal of the muted greenery. Most of the plants are native to Ontario, such as the ferns that soften the edges of the gravel paths. They have been collected from the wild as tiny plants on well-travelled trails, where their future was in jeopardy. Native willows, pines and birches also provide background. The centrepiece of the garden is the bridge, which traverses the pond and leads to a handsome wood gate at the rear of the lot, now weathered and partially hidden by shrubs and trees. It looks ancient and reassuring, and hints at vistas beyond. On either side of the gate sit moon-viewing benches made from stone which was salvaged from the demolition of a Thunder Bay municipal building; from the benches the new and waning moons can be seen. On the other side of the gate stretches the city property. "After midnight on a moonlit night this is my chosen spot," says Patrick. "It's beautiful, almost silent when there's an east wind to carry away the sounds of the highway."

Above: *One of Patrick's moon-viewing benches.*

Colour other than green is incidental in Japanese gardens, but there are some seasonal highs. Patrick's crabapple trees duplicate the show put on by cherry blossoms in Japan. In spring, the rich, rose blossoms of 'Red Jade' add colour next to the house, followed by dark plum foliage all sum-

hile Patrick Kelly's ability to move rocks and make interesting benches with them is amazing, his ability to grow raspberries is astounding. His canes, summer-bearing, came from a neighbour more than thirty years ago and were moved to the Kellys' present home when they built it; the variety name has long been forgotten. Two recommended summer-bearing varieties are 'Newburg' for large berries, or 'Taylor', the ultimate choice for flavour.

Patrick is an organic gardener and doesn't use chemical fertilizers in the raspberry patch. The canes grow in a raised bed of their own, in which the initial soil was prepared with well-rotted compost. The bed gets a top dressing of compost annually, and each spring Patrick prunes out the old canes to the ground and supports new ones inside a post-and-wire support structure. When mowing starts, Patrick mulches the canes with grass clippings (he doesn't use herbicides on the lawn). The grass mulch, never more than two inches (five centimetres) deep, not only prevents moisture loss from the soil during summer but also keeps weeds down and surface roots cool, and provides the plants with nutrition as the grass rots.

mer long. The branches frame the view into the garden from the windows of the rear sunroom, and provide perches for the birds that frequent the garden all year.

Concrete lanterns made by Patrick lead the way through the garden. They, too, have taken on a patina of age. They have been placed with thought and surrounded by plants and small rocks for a natural look. Spreading juniper is used extensively, and gives the feeling of gently rolling hills as pleasing to the eye as grass—and easier to maintain. Near the patio an old Oriental pot serves as a *tsukubai*; from a bamboo spout water trickles into the hollow of the stone. In the traditional Japanese tea ceremony it

***Above:** Junipers, water lilies, Japanese lanterns, and a bridge are set off by the colours of fall.*

was customary to wash one's hands in the *tsukubai* before joining the host in the teahouse.

The pond is full of water lilies that are almost ancient—they're thirty-four years old and came from the Kellys' former garden. Each summer, the water lilies reward them for good care with pink, white and copper blooms nestled among flat green lily pads. "I don't know what varieties they are," says Patrick. "They were given to us as divisions long ago by another gardener." Every winter the pots are lifted and kept in a cool part of the basement where the temperature doesn't exceed fifty-nine degrees Fahrenheit (fifteen degrees Celsius).

Above: Iris sibirica.

Right: *A flowering crabapple frames this cool spring scene.*

Irises are among Patrick's most prized plants, Siberian and old cultivars of *Iris germanica*, or flag iris. A favourite one has burgundy and yellow blossoms. "But I can't tell you its name either," he laughs, "since it was a division from a friend."

Raspberries are also favourite plants. They grow in Patrick's well-organized vegetable patch tucked out of sight behind a tall hedge. The raspberries take up a nine- by twelve-foot (three- by four-metre) space, and grow to nine feet (three metres) tall; they, too, grew from a few canes cut from a neighbour's garden, where they had been planted in 1930! Patrick says they still produce "like crazy."

The vegetables grow in four raised beds with concrete pathways between them; this is the way the Chinese have grown vegetables for centuries. The soil is never walked on, and all the work can be done from the paths.

Compost is used liberally on the whole garden, and the Kellys have two bins on the go all the time. Patrick also adds cow manure to the garden every four years. "Our soil is sandy loam and it requires constant fertilizing," he says. "But I never use commercial fertilizer." He has great success with peas, particularly 'Lincoln'; and he successfully grows staples like carrots, beans and potatoes.

"I watched my grandfather and my father garden, and I guess I stored it all away in my memory for future use," says Patrick. "I never consider gardening work, but a labour of love. My wife calls me a romantic, and she's usually right."

The Heritage Garden

of John MacKeen

Small gardens hold a tremendous amount of charm. They're also fun to work in because there's only enough space for the gardener's special choices. And so it is with the colonial-style garden of John and Anne MacKeen, a small, picket-fenced find tucked into the shore of Passamaquoddy Bay in St. Andrews, New Brunswick.

The garden surrounds a delightful grey-painted clapboard home that John built himself on another property. Just over eleven years ago, John, a professor of English literature at the University of New Brunswick in Saint John, and Anne, a painter, semi-retired to the present location, and brought their one-and-a-half-storey home with them.

Photographs by Canapress/Alvin Corbett

Above: *An old-fashioned peony in all its glory.*

The property, once part of the railroad that brought people to the grand resort of St. Andrews, sits on a ledge of solid rock, and John realized that raised beds were the only way to get enough good soil into the garden to make things grow successfully. He demolished an old stone maintenance shed and built beds against the house with the lumber and stones. Finding good soil, however, was a challenge. John located some sandy soil nearby, brought it in and mixed it with seaweed and compost. (Seaweed, a valuable source of garden fertilizer, second only to well-rotted farmyard manure, is still a major part of John's composting. Because it's moist when added, it helps speed up the process.) "I guess I mixed less than half organic matter with the soil," he says. "I was surprised to find out how little was needed, because that soil looked awfully sandy." He's since built a third raised bed, a vegetable garden at the side of the house that is fast being overtaken with ornamentals. Raised beds and sandy soil have the

***Previous page:** A sheltered patio framed with flowers catches the summer sun; honeysuckle* (Lonicera x 'Dropmore Scarlet') *and roses climb beside the house.*

advantage of good drainage and quick warming in spring. "They also extend the growing season in the fall, especially on the sheltered south and west sides of the house," says John. There's a downside, however: during periods of drought—which have been more common in recent seasons—a lot of watering is necessary. To that end, John has placed large oak rain barrels at each corner of the house and around Anne's studio, a stone's throw from the back door.

Salt spray from Passamaquoddy Bay can also be a problem. It burns foliage. To counteract its effect John has sheltered the whole garden with a variety of unusual hedges and trees. Highbush cranberry (*Viburnum trilobum*), a native shrub of the area, grows in great billowing harmony with the white picket fence, which gives the garden a sense of enclosure. The white and cream lacecap flowers are sweetly scented in early summer; later on, the abundant fruit attracts birds to the garden. A fine old oak shades Anne's studio and shelters the garden, and its leaves feed the compost pile in fall. The thorns of a gooseberry hedge (*Ribes uva-crispa*) discourage all living creatures from trying to pass through it. Gooseberries are not widely grown in Canada, but their fruit is delicious. In the MacKeens' garden they perform triple duty: a hedge and windbreak, canned fruit for winter pies, and a lure for birds.

Because it's exposed to the elements, the vegetable garden required more protection than the beds near the house. John chose the old-fashioned and hardy Turkestan rose (*Rosa rugosa*) as a hedging material. "It more than survives, it thrives in these gusty seaside conditions. It's even been covered by the tide on occasion." It has tough but good-looking green foliage all summer, and the large, single, deep-rose flowers in spring are sweetly scented. In late summer it has attractive red rose hips.

The ever-decreasing variety of vegetables includes beans, beets, green onions and, says John, "excellent carrots. They like the sandy soil." John's recent passion is for azaleas from seed, in particular *Azalea mollis* 'Exbury' hybrids, which he buys from Sutton's Seeds in the U.K. Exbury is a large estate in the south of England owned by the Rothschild family, who raise a fine collection of rhododendrons and azaleas. "I should have started my azalea hobby years ago," John says with a twinkle in his eye. "It'll be ages before my babies bloom."

Below: *John tends his azalea seedlings.*

John MacKeen is proud of his Scottish heritage and grows many varieties of heather, which do extremely well in his garden. A particularly fine form, *Calluna vulgaris*, he grew from a sprig brought back from Scotland by a friend, who had picked it on Rannoch Moor. The cutting took to his garden immediately, and from the new plant he's taken many more cuttings to give to friends. John also grows native heathers and other members of the Ericaceae family, such as the low-growing native cranberries and blueberries, and Labrador tea (*Ledum groenlandicum*), a shrub somewhat like a small rhododendron, with off-white flowers.

rowing azaleas from seed takes patience, says John MacKeen. It's not the germination process, or even growing the seedlings to the planting-out stage. It's waiting for the bloom that requires a patient nature: it often takes five years.

John plants seeds in a moist peat mix in the warmth of the house in late February to early March, depending on when the seed order arrives. The seeds are very fine, so he scatters them on the surface and covers them only with a dark cloth until they show signs of germinating—usually in two weeks or less. They are grown to transplanting stage on a cool (fifty-five degrees Fahrenheit/thirteen degrees Celsius) well-lit windowsill without artificial lights. Once the tiny seedlings are large enough to handle, usually in June, they are transplanted into individual pots and grown on in a peaty raised bed custom-made for them.

They are kept well watered and shaded from hot sun—when the Atlantic fog doesn't do it naturally. In five to seven years or so, they bloom, perhaps with a completely new coloured form.

Sheep laurel (*Kalmia angustifolia*), a smallish shrub with exquisite clusters of purple-to-crimson flowers in early summer, is another member of the Ericaceae family, this one a Maritime gem.

John brought favourite plants as well as the house from the original site. "There are many links with past generations in this garden," he says, and cites a fine Russian olive (*Eleagnus angustifolia*) in the heather garden. It's a hardy deciduous tree of great merit, with silvery foliage and sweetly scented silver-yellow flowers in summer. "This specimen came from my great-grandmother's garden in Cape Breton," he says. He points to a Dutch honeysuckle (*Lonicera periclymenum*) climbing up the house. "It grew in an aunt's garden, and those two unnamed roses, the white one and the cinnamon one, are from my St. John River farm." Of course, many other plants in the perennial beds were trades from local gardeners. The beds are crowded, as one would expect of a cottage-style garden, and full of old-

Left: Bluebells of Scotland (Campanula rotundifolia).

Below: *John's cottage garden features old-fashioned perennials such as garden pinks* (Dianthus plumarius), *daisies* (Chrysanthemum x superbum), *and delphiniums.*

fashioned favourites. Blue delphiniums, which thrive on the soft New Brunswick air, grow next to *Trollius europaeus*, those wonderful, non-invasive, giant perennial buttercups. Nearby, showing off like quaint bouquets, are pyrethrums (*Chrysanthemum coccineum*), with their rose-pink flowers and bright yellow centres. Bright red Maltese cross (*Lychnis chalcedonica*) stand in erect bunches throughout the beds, softened by the nodding bonnet-like heads of columbines (*Aquilegia caerulea*) in varying shades and colours. Bordering the garden is another old-country favourite, annual candytuft (*Iberis umbellata*), with its small clumps of white, pink and mauve flowers. The candytuft is a volunteer that comes up every year. John waits until it germinates and transplants those he wants to the border.

The winter winds can be a problem, and the intermittent snowfalls, although often heavy, don't guarantee protection. So right after the first frost, John covers tender plants with pine needles. "They're light and they shed the water, plus they're so filled with resin they last for years. If you let them dry out before raking them up in spring, they can be stored in bags for the following winter."

The Mediterranean Garden

of David Dombowsky & Linda Dunlop

Photographs by Michael Brauer

Gardeners who visit the large estate and castle gardens of Europe always marvel at the favourable microclimates created by the walls that encase them, and the walls' aesthetic appeal seldom goes unnoticed. In Saskatoon, Linda Dunlop and David Dombowsky, who have visited a few exotic places in their time, have created a superb walled garden in the best Mediterranean tradition, using hundreds of stones gathered from the surrounding countryside.

Like the European variety, their wall provides privacy and charm, plus benefits invaluable in the Zone 2 climate: it traps heat, lengthening the season at each end; it acts as a windbreak; and it catches snow, which blankets the garden in winter and protects many plants, such as the hardy hibiscus, that might not otherwise survive.

***Above:** A custom-built gate clothed with Virginia creeper* (Parthenocissus quinquefolia) *welcomes visitors to the garden.*

The badly neglected house and yard presented a challenge when the couple purchased it in 1979. Linda, an interior designer, took on the task of renovating the interior and designing an addition to the house, and David took on the yard, which he transformed into a formal garden. After he cleared away the weeds, he removed the cracked garden paths, the fallen-down shed and the metal clothesline. But two features caused him some headaches: the concrete children's paddling pool and a double-rung steel fence enclosing the north and east perimeters of the garden.

Because it was anchored in a concrete base three feet (one metre) deep, the fence proved impossible to move. Enclosing it in a stone wall seemed the only solution. "I've always been drawn to stone structures," says David. "During travel for my job, I've seen Hadrian's Wall, the Great

Previous page: *Blue morning glories* (Ipomoea tricolor *'Heavenly Blue'), corn and marigolds complement David's magnificent stone wall.*

Wall of China, the Taj Mahal. Walls are wonderful things."

He talks about how he built the six-foot (two-metre) wall as if it were an easy task, but Linda reminds him it took four summers to complete. Building it was only half the work—first, the rocks had to be collected. Early each summer they'd rent a truck or a trailer and drive into the countryside in search of interesting specimens. A large load came from an uncle's farm; a friend donated a few truckloads. Their goal was to have a large stock on hand by early June and then build like mad all summer. "The rock hunting was actually great fun," says David. "I always had my rock hammer handy in the trunk, and if we were out on a Sunday drive and spotted a good rock, I'd split off a chunk." Linda had chosen a Mediterranean-style pink stucco finish for the house, so they looked for rocks with veins of warm russets, pinks and purples. They are, however, sensitive wall-builders, so for the outer layer of the foot-thick (thirty-centimetre) wall, they chose grey and off-white stones to complement their neighbour's white house with black trim. Some of the smaller specimens built into the wall have sentimental value: they were collected on their travels, from such places as Mount Masada in Israel. David took the same inspired approach with the children's pool, incorporating it into the overall design so that it looks like an extension of the wall.

Linda and David were new to gardening when they embarked on their lot renovation, so they enlisted the help of a friend, Robert D. Brown (who now teaches landscape architecture at Ontario's Guelph University), to help plan it. He suggested a wide, welcoming path entering the garden and a grid of four formal beds containing vegetables, flowers and herbs. A magnificent steel gate painted dark green, with a tracing of Virginia creeper on top, beckons the visitor into the garden. It's reminiscent of the lovely old wrought-iron gates at the entrances of European estates—and for a reason: Linda designed it to follow the style and it was hand-made by a local ironworker who learned his craft in Germany. The bricks on the pathway are a combination of old and new; some of them came from the Capitol Theatre, one of Saskatoon's oldest theatres, demolished despite a local heritage building group's dedicated efforts to save it. Because of heavy winter frost, brick isn't often used in prairie gardens, but these have stood up well. Those that tend to flake are treated with a sealant. David arranged them in pleasing herringbone and running bond patterns, alternating new and old bricks. "It hoses off easily and is never slippery," says David, which would not be true in wetter climates.

Above: Clematis jackmanii *and white petunias create a restful composition.*

The garden's heavy clay soil needs constant work to be kept friable and full of nutrients. Because of the lack of space, Linda and David don't compost, but they're able to get well-rotted cow manure to add to the garden annually, and when needed they also add sand and peat moss. In the vegetable beds, the two quadrants closest to the garden wall, they grow varieties they like best. Tomatoes, for example, are staked on rebar painted dark green to match the garden gate; as they grow the side shoots are carefully removed and the leaves trimmed so the plants fit the formality of the garden. Corn thrives in the reflected heat of the wall. David is particularly fond of the strong leaves and the

hen David Dombowsky and Linda Dunlop moved into their new home they inherited an unsightly concrete wading pool in the corner of the garden. Not only was it full of junk, it was going to be almost impossible to remove. David decided to transform it into a pond that would carry out the Mediterranean theme of the rest of the walled garden. It's a clever disguise that works because of David's skillful way with rocks.

The pool, approximately six and a half by ten feet (two by three metres), has a rocked-in wall that echoes the tall stone wall protecting the garden. Above the pool David installed a two-tiered waterfall, using large rocks for the water course and leaving pockets for spreading junipers to soften the scene. The water pipe that feeds the falls from the recirculating pump in the pond is attached to the wall, so it's easy to reach if maintenance is required. During the summer, Virginia creeper hides it, so it appears the water is pouring forth from the vine.

The gentle sound of falling water adds magic to the atmosphere of the garden during the summer months, as do the gorgeous koi in the pond. The koi spend the winter in indoor aquariums, when the pool and pipes are drained for winter. In colder climates, lining the pond with a good thickness of straw also helps prevent cracking.

shape of the corn plant, so they're left in the ground all winter to provide architectural interest. "They also make a nice natural fence," says David. Brussels sprouts, another vegetable seldom grown in the short prairie summer, produces delicious sprouts late into the season, and they taste even better after they've been touched by a bit of early frost. With the improved soil conditions, carrots also do well; Linda and David love eating them fresh-picked and raw.

"No salad is complete without arugula," says Linda, so it's a necessity in the herb garden. Parsley makes an attractive edging plant, continuing the Mediterranean theme, and another surprise is rosemary. "We prefer its flavour to sage," says Linda. They nurture it carefully near the wall. Basil is also a staple in the herb bed, where it grows lushly and happily.

Perennial plants thrive well on the Prairies because of the usually guaranteed winter snow cover. Linda and David grow 'Morden Pink' lythrum, the sterile form of purple loosestrife; several old-fashioned bearded irises; and *Campanula carpatica*, both the blue and white forms, which form small mounds that gently overflow the edge of the brick path. Spanking white marguerites abound and intermingle with the golden, similarly daisy-like flowers of heliopsis.

Annual flowers grow quickly in the long, sunny summer days, and they are well represented in the garden. "But our tastes are evolving and we're getting more into perennials all the time," says David. Marigolds are long-time favourite annuals, as are the beautiful tuberous begonias, the blossoms of which Linda floats in a rose bowl indoors. She's had great success overwintering the tubers for several years now. She also grows annual carnations and asters to use in flower arrangements.

The wall itself supports more plants. On it David has espaliered a cherry tree, which blends with the uneven, pleasing contours of the stones. A native form of the hardy Manitoba grape produces countless small bunches of grapes; they're too sour to eat, but they look pretty in late summer and the foliage provides good fall colour. The seldom-grown but hardy kiwi vine (*Actinidia arguta*) has yet to produce fruit; it's not the fuzzy New Zealand kiwi sold at supermarkets and greengrocers, but a much smaller variety—and just as tasty, especially if it's left on the vines as late in the season as possible. Honeysuckle 'Dropmore Scarlet' also hugs the wall, attracting many hummingbirds with its orange-red blossoms in early summer. Unfortunately, the purple *Clematis jackmanii* David had trained over a trellis on the front of the house has died, but it will soon be replaced with another hardier form.

Left: *The old children's wading pool, converted to a pond, now provides the cool sound of water during the hot prairie summer.*

Below: *This scene of prolific growth shows what a walled Mediterranean-style prairie garden can produce.*

The garden is nearly complete now, allowing David and Linda some time to savour its colours and smells from the raised brick patio that opens off the house. Like the rest of the garden, it is protected by the stone wall, allowing it to be used earlier in spring and later in fall. But the couple is not likely to spend too much time admiring the view. "I'm Polish," says David. "Gardening is part of my heritage."

Linda says gardening is more than genetic, it's a respite from their busy daily lives. "It's both aesthetic and utilitarian," she says. "I think living in harmony with nature is good for the soul. And after a long cold Saskatchewan winter, neither of us can wait to get outside again. We like planning the garden and trying new plants. Watching the vegetable seeds or the first flowers come into bloom is akin to witnessing a birth. It's exciting! And when it comes down to it, we like eating our veggies, both for their superior flavour and our own sense of accomplishment."

The Country Garden

of Kathryn McHolm

Photographs by Christopher Dew

Sixty-three miles (ninety-five kilometres) east of the hustle and bustle of Metropolitan Toronto lies the tiny, sleepy village of Welcome. On warm summer evenings the soft darkness enfolds one and the sound of friendly insects fills the air. It's a perfect setting for Kathryn McHolm, an artist, painter and papermaker, who makes her living from the bounty of her garden, and an instinctive gardener who likes to let nature take its course.

Kathryn works from the Bric-a-Brac Shack, a small, weathered and vine-covered building at the back of her garden. Inside, the air is filled with the sweet scent of new-mown hay and other heady perfumes. Nosegays of herbs and flowers hang from the rafters, jars of seed pods and petals line the shelves, bolts of satin and lace ribbon and hand-woven baskets tumble over worktables. It's a beguiling place, almost hypnotic in effect.

Above: *In the cutting garden, golden annual yarrow* (Achillea filipendula) *is backed by the soft pastels of larkspur* (Consolida ambigua).

Kathryn was raised in Welcome but moved to nearby Port Hope when she grew up. The tiny shack had always been there, part of the property adjacent to her family's farm, but Kathryn didn't pay it much attention until she painted a water colour of the neighbouring farmhouse a few years back, and in her mind's eye saw it surrounded by a garden. In 1986, she bought the property and began to make her vision a reality.

There have always been gardeners in the McHolm family, and Kathryn has an almost genetic sense of the environment around her. She allows much of her garden to just happen, with a helping hand from her. "My garden is very transient," she says. "Plants that started in one area find their way to other beds. From year to year the change can

Previous page: *A mixture of cultivated and wild flowers blooms all summer long in Kathryn's garden.*

be dramatic—visitors often comment on it. But I'm not totally permissive—if the plants get out of hand, a tug now and then keeps them under control."

The main garden runs along the south side and the front of the present house, and Kathryn feels sure it was part of the original garden. It contains many wonderful old plants—sweetly scented lemon lilies (*Hemerocallis thunbergii*), much daintier than most modern daylily hybrids; unknown cultivars of peonies, probably from the early species of *Paeonia lactiflora*, again with a good perfume; and narcissus that have naturalized and are welcome harbingers of spring. In what must once have been the kitchen garden grow rhubarb and Jerusalem artichokes (*Helianthus tuberosus*), which pop up all over, their tall stems capped by small sunflower-like daisies.

Decades-old shrubs include an early form of mock orange (*Philadelphus coronarius*), which is covered in early summer with large clusters of white blooms heavy with the scent of orange blossoms. A flowering quince and an old rose—"probably 'Maiden's Blush'," says Kathryn—flourish. Near the Bric-a-Brac Shack grow three old apple trees: Bellflower, a variety with large red-cheeked fruit; a MacIntosh thought to be from the original stock; and a Melba, planted by the last owner, who lived on the property from 1926 until 1986.

The garden is divided into areas by loosely arranged cedar hedges, cherry trees bursting with blossoms each spring, and a shrub island with flowering currant and the old quince. Like all old-fashioned gardens remembered from one's youth, this one is alive with the sound of birds, the buzzing of bees, and the lazy flutter of butterflies.

The soil on the property offers tantalizing hints of its past. On the south side, where the original garden probably stood, it's clay loam; on the other, the soil is light and sandy. "I think this is where the foundations of the first house stood," says Kathryn. Near the present house lies a bank she feels was used as a dumping or refuse area; while digging in it she's unearthed old bottles, bricks and bits of metal.

Below: *The scent of dried flowers lingers all year long in the drying barn.*

Kathryn has a talent for weaving baskets, and she's taken it a step further by using grapevines to make a charming old-fashioned wattle fence to separate her front yard from the road. She also uses branching twigs as natural trellises for low-growing vining plants, and encourages climbing hydrangeas (*Hydrangea anomala*), scarlet trumpet vine (*Campsis radicans*) and Virginia creeper to grow over the dead or dying branches of old trees.

Composting is an important practice in Kathryn's garden. She uses compost as top-dressing throughout the garden and digs it in where the soil is poor. In her new vegetable bed she is experimenting with the leaf mould that's so abundant in the area. Her natural gardening practices extend to pest and disease control as well. "I'm lucky that few seem to bother my garden," she says. "But one patch of Jerusalem artichokes seems vulnerable to powdery mildew. For that I use

athryn McHolm's handmade wattle fence is not just attractive—it's a conversation piece in her garden and an innovative way to use grapevine prunings. Kathryn installed six-foot (two-metre) posts about two feet (sixty centimetres) deep and two feet (sixty centimetres) apart in the soil across the front of her garden, then wove the grapevine lengths between the posts, spacing them so it's possible to see through the finished fence. Kathryn suggests that any pliable woody vines or stems may be used—for example, long shoots pruned from kiwi, wisteria and bittersweet—and adds that the fence is easy to repair by weaving in new vines to replace rotted ones. If a support post rots, it can be removed and a new post threaded down through the vines and pounded into place with a mallet. A wattle fence never needs painting, it provides a windbreak and it gives a private background to a beautiful country garden.

good old-fashioned sulphur." She blasts aphids off with a sharp jet of water from the hose, and if they persist she uses an insecticidal soap. She hand picks and kills the little worms that sometimes find the roses, or washes them off with a strong stream from the hose.

Kathryn grows everything she uses in her dried-flower arrangements, wreaths and wedding bouquets—plants like strawflowers, statice, larkspur, bachelor's buttons and sky-blue annual *Salvia patens*. Many are volunteers, but many she starts herself each year from seed. A few years ago she had access to a friend's greenhouse, but now she raises her seedlings successfully in the house under lights.

Kathryn does make some concessions to a high-tech age. She carries a cellular phone everywhere—even in her garden basket with her pruning shears—and she uses a chipper-shredder to reduce prunings (after they've been carefully scrutinized as possible vine supports) into mulch, which she also uses for pathways. But her garden is peaceful and appealing because of its ties with another age. "I like having plants my grandmother and my great-grandmother had," she says. "All the old favourites like hollyhocks, peonies, daylilies, roses and irises. But I also grow things some people consider roadside weeds because they look great in arrangements—giant thistles and goldenrod, for example."

One of Kathryn's more ambitious recent projects was a rock garden and pond along the north side of her house. All told, she moved in about eleven tons (eleven tonnes) of Ontario limestone, and it took from May till the end of October a couple of years ago to finish. Most of the rocks found a home in the rock garden, but some wait in a pile behind her studio for her to dream up another project.

Winter doesn't bring much respite for Kathryn—then she teaches classes in papermaking and basket weaving, and paints water colours. "Even in winter my garden inspires me. It gives me materials for wreaths, baskets and papermaking, and ideas to paint," she says. "I get great pleasure from it, but best of all I like to share it with others."

Left: *Kathryn's innovative hand-woven fence.*

Below: *Marguerites, zinnias and calendulas are almost ready for cutting and drying.*

The Island Garden

of Sandy & Des Kennedy

Photographs by Paul Bailey

Sandy and Des Kennedy's charming garden on Denman Island, one of the northern Gulf Islands tucked into the sheltered waters of the Strait of Georgia, has a fairy-tale look and a lush, almost rampant feeling that makes one think Mother Nature might have grown it herself. But developing the naturally forested eleven-acre (4.45-hectare) site was no mean feat. As Des says: "How do you go about replacing one of nature's own lovely wild gardens with a manmade one?"

The Kennedys' philosophy of gardening is to work closely with nature—and on a strict budget. "We designed the garden to fit the natural woodland around it," says Des. This philosophy extends to the fences and other garden structures, all made from materials found on the property. And they've encouraged wildlife to inhabit the garden by creating ponds, rock piles and natural bushy areas for the birds. "But it hasn't been easy," says Des. "Our gardening tends to be labour intensive because we try to do better with less."

Above: *An oriental poppy unfolds like tissue paper.*

The Kennedys bought the land in 1975 and started clearing it at once. Not all of the property is cultivated but an area around the wooden cottage—which they built from local materials—is filled with flowers. Once the house was livable they started on the garden.

Because the land drops in gently rolling slopes to a small stream, and the surrounding evergreen forest is filled with softly rounded shapes, Des and Sandy knew the garden had to be curved and non-angular. None of the paths, fences or walls have a sharp angle; all curve gently, fitting perfectly with the terrain and leading one's eye to the forest beyond.

Des and Sandy soon realized the location had another advantage: with

***Previous page:** Terraced beds support many colourful drought-tolerant plants: daisies* (Chrysanthemum leucanthemum)*, Scotch thistle* (Onopordom acanthium)*, and lamb's ears* (Stachys byzantina) *are backed with colourful delphiniums and foxgloves* (Digitalis purpurea).

no nearby road and no passersby, they were free to create a landscape for themselves alone. A large portion was left as grass pasture dotted with native trees, and an enclosure to be viewed from the cottage was planned. "We're surrounded by forest, so all our views are short," says Des. "It seemed important to have a variety of sightlines. Some of them enhance the sense of the enclosure, of its intimacy and distance from the outer world, while others expand the horizon and prevent claustrophobia."

But the enclosure needed protection from the local deer that roam the area. Des and Sandy built a fence and gate using wood poles set aside when the property was cleared, and purchased inexpensive stucco wire to deerproof the fence. The stucco wire is now clothed with heritage roses through which the deer can be seen grazing on the green grass beyond.

Summer's drought conditions on B.C.'s Gulf Islands coupled with the sandy soil meant that organic matter was a necessity if the garden was to be a success. There was a lot of vegetation to compost. "We usually have several compost heaps going at one time," says Des. "We use garden and kitchen refuse, plus loads of seaweed from the beach and the sludge from our composting privy. Occasionally we buy a dump-truck load of commercial compost, which is made from salmon-farm corpses and wood chips. We also gather heaps of maple leaves each autumn."

The garden is terraced and interlaced with beautiful sandstone walls and paths, and the beds overflow with colourful annuals and perennials all season long. At first the uneven terrain seemed a problem to be solved, particularly one small hill just west of the house. But when a gardening friend visited one day and commented that he'd give anything for a hill like that, Des and Sandy took another look. "Suddenly I saw it terraced with rocks," says Des. "It was a brief moment of inspiration, but it was followed by months of back-cracking work."

Below: *Delphiniums and double poppies make a fine combination, announcing the advent of summer.*

Local sandstone in a warm brown colour is the bedrock of the garden. Small flat pieces were used for the retaining walls, an alcove, and for the half-moon patio at the front door. Larger pieces form flagstone paths like those in old English gardens, interplanted with various species of thyme whose fragrance fills the air when they're walked on. "In the warm spring sun, the pathways are favourite basking places for the garter snakes who patrol the garden in search of slugs," says Des. "The stone is beautiful in winter, too, when the rains make them glisten. With the foliage gone, the paths *are* the garden—they give it a sense of symmetry and solidity."

Native and cultivated plants easily harmonize in the garden. An old cedar stump is clothed with native huckleberry (*Vaccinium ovatum*), a plant lovely in all seasons but especially in winter, when its bare, reddish-tinged

Most of Des and Sandy Kennedy's pioneer-style garden structures are admirable, but the deer fence that doubles as an arbour is intriguing in its design. Denman Island swarms with blacktail deer and fencing the garden was a necessity. The upright support posts of the fence are hand-split cedar rails seven feet (two metres) high; two feet (sixty centimetres) is firmly embedded in concrete below ground. Because the posts are cedar, no preservative was used. T-bars were added at right-angles to each post top to support two more split rails that run horizontally above to support climbing plants. To keep the deer out, the lower part of the open area is filled with inexpensive galvanized stucco wire, sold in rolls approximately six feet (two metres) wide. It is strong and much less expensive than chainlink fencing. It allows Des and Sandy to see both the rolling meadow-like lawn beyond the fence and the deer that look longingly through the wire at the garden. A single wire runs midway between the top of the stucco wire and the upper rail to discourage the deer from trying to jump through.

branches glow. Native bleeding heart (*Dicentra formosa*) sends up its finely cut foliage early in the spring, and soon shows off its dainty, drooping spikes of magenta-pink flowers. Miner's-lettuce (*Montia perfoliata*), a green favoured by pioneers, is abundant along the forest edge early in the year and the large spring-green foliage of vanilla leaf (*Achlys triphylla*) clothes the forest floor. The forest is also home to many sword ferns (*Polystichum munitum*) that were moved there from the land where the house and garden now stand.

In the fenced garden, old-fashioned perennials and roses are interspersed with native plants. Des and Sandy grow over eighty varieties of roses, mostly old varieties. "We grow them for the scent, and the voluptuousness of their June bloom," says Des. "We also grow several dozen peonies for the same reason." Herbaceous perennials dominate the garden: delphiniums do extremely well without much fussing, and they attract butterflies as well as contributing to the dried flower arrangements that help get the Kennedys through the winter. Oriental poppies (*Papaver orientale*) unfold their tissue-paper petals in the early summer sun; hostas and Solomon's seal (*Polygonatum* x *hybridum*) grace shadier areas.

In summer, drought-tolerant plants are almost a necessity, since the Kennedys rely on natural rainfall to water their garden. Lamb's ears (*Stachys byzantina*) form great soft grey cushions that spill over the rock walls: ornamental catmint (*Nepeta* x *faassenii*) forms purple-blue mounds throughout the garden. Oregano thrives as happily as if it were home in Greece, and adds to the summer's perfume. Artemisia continues the silver-blue theme in many areas, combined with the giant silver thistle (*Onopordon acanthium*); in many seasons it grows ten feet (three metres) tall.

Late in the summer, the golden rays of several rudbeckia take over the garden, along with that reliable cottage-garden plant *Sedum spectabile* 'Autumn Joy'; bees and butterflies revel in its dense, dark-pink flower heads. Other favourite fall plants are Michaelmas daisies and many forms of *Aster novi-belgii*.

Scattered through the garden are great stands of purple foxglove (*Digitalis purpurea*), an introduced—and very happy—plant in British Columbia. In spring, the tall spikes of large bell-shaped flowers are alive with the sound of bees. Later, clumps of another introduced resident, the cheerful yellow and white oxeye daisy (*Chrysanthemum leucanthemum*), brighten the beds. Orange California poppies, annuals that reseed themselves year after year, are also well established. "They pop up on their own and carry on without much care from us," says Des.

The Kennedys work hard and love their garden. "It's a joint undertaking that nurtures and sustains our relationship," says Des. "And it's good for us—it gets us outdoors most of the year, and fosters a connection with the natural world. It's grand exercise for our minds as well, because we live far from the stimulations of the city. Our garden provides excitement right at our doorstep."

Left: *A flagstone path edged with California poppies (*Eschscholzia californica*), lady's mantle (*Alchemilla mollis*), and a variety of herbs leads invitingly to the forest beyond.*

Below: *Exuberant floral displays surround Des and Sandy's cottage in early summer.*

The Harmonious Garden

of Brian Folmer

Photographs by Christopher Dew

It isn't that Brian Folmer dislikes grass; he'd just had enough of cutting it. Every weekend he'd get the mower out of the shed on his parents' half-acre (.2-hectare) lot just outside the tiny village of Chepstow, Ontario, and spend half the day cutting and trimming. But somehow, all that manicured expanse of green just didn't seem worth the effort, and it looked like every other farm property for miles around. So with his mother, Agnes, Brian decided it was time to put in a real garden, something that might be a bit more work but would provide them with more enjoyment. Gradually, the two of them took out all the turf, and have created a garden that is a neighbourhood show place, an oasis of colour among rippling fields of grain.

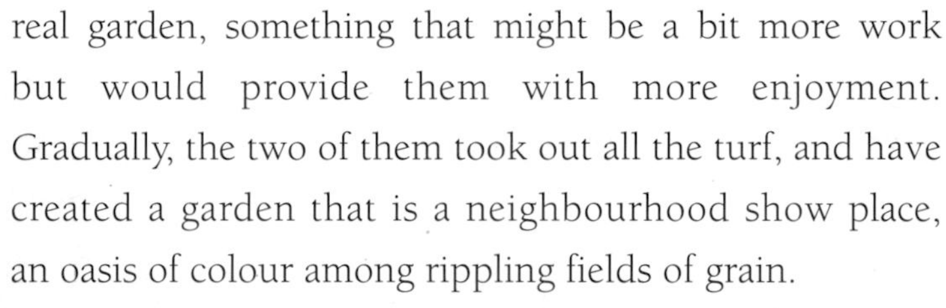

Above: *A winding gravel path skirts a bed of thyme, which provides a colour echo for spectacular* Lilium regale.

Brian's experiment in gardening has had a happy result: it led him to enroll in the University of Guelph's landscape architecture program, and currently he's an associate member of the Ontario Landscape Association. Brian has become one of those fortunate souls who's turned an absorbing hobby into a career.

His goal was to make a fulsome garden that would rival the British style, one made up of small themed areas joined by architectural elements such as a pathway or an arbour, or connected by trailing ground covers. Within the lot he's created many small vignettes with an unerring eye for combining colours and textures, among them a rose garden, a rock garden, the perennial beds, and a vegetable plot. "The garden is an extension of the house to us," he says. "We try to live in it to the fullest—lots of tables and chairs on the porch and a deck add to its use. And we're always experimenting with plants. We're in Zone 5, but we

***Previous page:** Water lilies and the floating water hyacinth* Eichhornia crassipes *create a cool water view.*

bend the rules where plant hardiness is concerned—plants can't read the hardiness map!" The garden has been planned for a balanced show of colour and texture from spring through fall, and during winter, an eye-pleasing mix of evergreens, textured barks and deciduous tree forms, with an accent of bright berries. Annuals are restricted to window boxes, planters and barrels on the porch and patio, leaving the permanent beds for perennials. "I like contrasts in flower colour," says Brian. "Combinations like orange Asiatic lilies with blue lavender, or red and yellow tulips for spring." He also favours plants with interesting foliage or pleasing fragrance, sometimes combining both features in one grouping, such as a planting of spear-leaved daylilies with an understorey of creeping thyme.

A stroll through the garden reveals a few surprises, such as the winter-flowering heathers (*Erica carnea*), which survive because of consistently good snow cover. "We're in the snow belt here," Brian says. "And that's an advantage. Sometimes the heathers are blooming away under the snow in late winter, and as soon as it melts, there they are." He grows the cultivars 'Springwood White' and 'Springwood Pink'. *Ginkgo biloba*, the ancient tree from China known as the maidenhair fern tree, is not usually hardy to Zone 5, but it thrives in his garden, as does the lovely yellow spring-flowering shrub *Kerria japonica*.

The soil, as you might well imagine in this rich farming area, is a good fertile loam, but during the construction of the house (it was built in 1970 on a section severed from Brian's grandfather's farm) most of the soil ended up in the front of the garden. But with good farmyard manure at hand, soil amendment is seldom a problem. In the back of the garden, where the topsoil was two or three inches (six centimetres) deep at best, Brian put in an alpine garden; behind it is the compost area, which is mined annually for top-dressing and new plantings.

In January the bones of the garden stand out to advantage, revealing pine, spruce, juniper, firs and several broadleaved evergreens, red and yellow osier dogwood (*Cornus stolonifera* and *C.s.* 'Flaviramea')—a dramatic choice for the snowy background—Amur maple (*Acer ginnala*) and serviceberry (*Amelanchier canadensis*). During warm spells in February, buttercup-yellow winter aconites (*Eranthis hyemalis*) peek through the snow and winter heathers announce that spring is on the way.

***Above:** An underplanting of blue grape hyacinths* (Muscari botryoides) *and spring bulbs around this white birch announce the season in Brian's garden.*

During April, witch hazel (*Hamamelis mollis*) and Cornelian cherries (*Cornus mas*) provide interest, with bright spring flowers carried on leafless branches. A parade of blossoms and textures advance the season, among the hardy *Rhododendron catawbiense* 'Nova Zelba' and *R. alba*. The beautiful white- and pink-flowered native redbud (*Cercis canadensis*) is used to advantage in the landscape, as is the star magnolia (*Magnolia stellata*), with off-white to pale-pink blossoms. Spring bulbs run riot, including crocus, *Iris reticulata*, scilla, tulips, daffodils and hyacinths.

Brian is greatly interested in plants native to Ontario, and he recently planted a small Carolinian woodland as one of his garden areas. Along with a redbud, it contains a native tulip tree (*Liriodendron tulipfera*) and a

One of Brian Folmer's secrets for making small gardens look larger than they are involves his love of textured plants. He uses various leaf textures and forms to create a pattern that pleases the eye. For example, beside a path, he suggests a mass of low, woolly thyme; about one and a half feet (forty-five centimetres) from the path's edge, he'd plant some bold hostas or heuchera, which will eventually be surrounded by the patch of creeping thyme; and toward the back of the bed, a couple of manageable shrubs, like serviceberry or Japanese quince. This could be accomplished in an area no more than five feet (1.5 metres) square and the various plant heights and leaf textures, coupled with their seasonal colour, would create the illusion of a much larger planting. This type of planting lends itself well to today's small townhome gardens.

fine specimen of red oak (*Quercus rubra*); in spring the white flowers and glaucous leaves of bloodroot (*Sanguinaria canadensis*) poke up through last season's dead leaves like little ballerinas dotting the woodland floor. Pale blue and white *Hepatica americana* complement the show. Because of his contacts in horticulture, finding unusual cultivars is not usually a problem for Brian, and he's incorporated native plants in many of his commercial projects. "I'm really encouraged by today's interest in native plants," he says. "Especially by Ontario nurserymen—they're growing many woody and perennial natives."

By high summer the garden is reaching its peak and looks like a large quilt, its colour blending to please the eye. Woolly thyme (*Thymus pseudolanuginosus*) is used extensively as a substitute for grass, for various reasons. "One of them is the memory of those days of mowing," Brian laughs. "But thyme is also drought tolerant, its soft grey downy foliage always looks good and it works well with almost every colour and texture." To prove another point, he walks across a springy clump and a pleasant aroma fills the air.

Daylilies are also very much in evidence through the garden. "Even when they're not blooming their foliage looks terrific," says Brian. He often combines them with lady's mantle (*Alchemilla mollis*), whose frothy chartreuse flowers combine hotly with the classic orange daylily (*Hemerocallis fulva*). Another strong combination is old-fashioned white shrub roses underplanted with lavender-blue catmint (*Nepeta* x *faassenii*).

Brian is a great believer in the importance of getting colours exactly right. "And gardeners should pay more attention to textures," he says. "You want to harmonize foliage shapes so they're pleasing throughout the growing season." He also thinks people should look more carefully at the colours and textures of the bare winter stems of deciduous shrubs, and capitalize on their beauty for the garden.

A planting of ground covers illustrates his point. A patch of common periwinkle (*Vinca minor*), which has lovely blue flowers early in the season and shiny dark green leaves all year, is interplanted with Indian strawberry (*Duchesnea indica*). Its tiny yellow flowers bloom about the same time as the periwinkle's blue ones, but it is the two types of foliage that work so well, like a weaving—one smooth and roundish, the other deeply toothed and slightly downy on the underside. "These can be weedy if they're not kept under control, but Mom and I bless the ground covers," says Brian. "They keep weeds down and cut down on our garden work."

Left: *Brian's garden reveals his skill in combining plants of different heights and leaf textures.*

Far left: *A carefully designed mosaic of colour includes lavender* (Lavandula angustifolia), *evening primrose* (Oenothera missouriensis), *Heuchera 'Palace Purple', snow-in-summer* (Cerastum tomentosum), Coreopsis grandiflora, *speedwell* (Veronica spicata) *and a variety of thymes.*

The Atlantic Garden

of Walter Ostrom

Photographs by Dan Callis

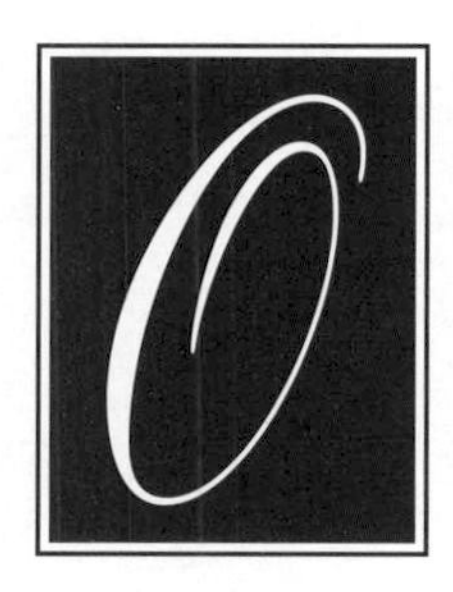

One of the tenets of gardening is that opportunities are always disguised as challenges. When they were faced with the dual challenge of creating a garden on near-bedrock battered by the ever-present winds of the Atlantic coast, Walter Ostrom and his wife, Elaine, realized it wasn't necessary to tame the craggy terrain but rather to accept it for its rugged beauty and strength. Today their garden in Indian Harbour, Nova Scotia, is a tapestry of colour and texture. Enhanced with free-form borders and linked with welcoming stone paths sloping gently away from the silver-grey house, it's a testimony to twenty years of allowing the terrain and climate to guide them.

Above: Lewisia tweedyi, *native to North America's western mountains, thrives on the Atlantic coast.*

The Ostroms' first humbling lesson came soon after they moved to their property. Walter, a professor of ceramics at the Nova Scotia College of Art and Design in Dalhousie, needed a studio for his work. He drew up plans based on old-fashioned pit greenhouses. To reduce heating bills—which Walter also hoped to do—the structures were to be half buried, but when a neighbour with a mechanical shovel began to dig the hole for the studio, he hit bedrock just eight inches (twenty centimetres) below the sod. Walter had to rethink his original plans. The result is a lovely stone and wood studio above ground. Highlighting the front is a raised scree bed, approximately forty inches (one metre) deep and wide, held in place by a dry stone wall. "I now have more respect for the Egyptians, having moved and placed every stone myself," Walter says.

Many of Walter's favourite plants thrive in this bed, a testimony to his love of gardening and eye for choice alpines, which include dwarf, pros-

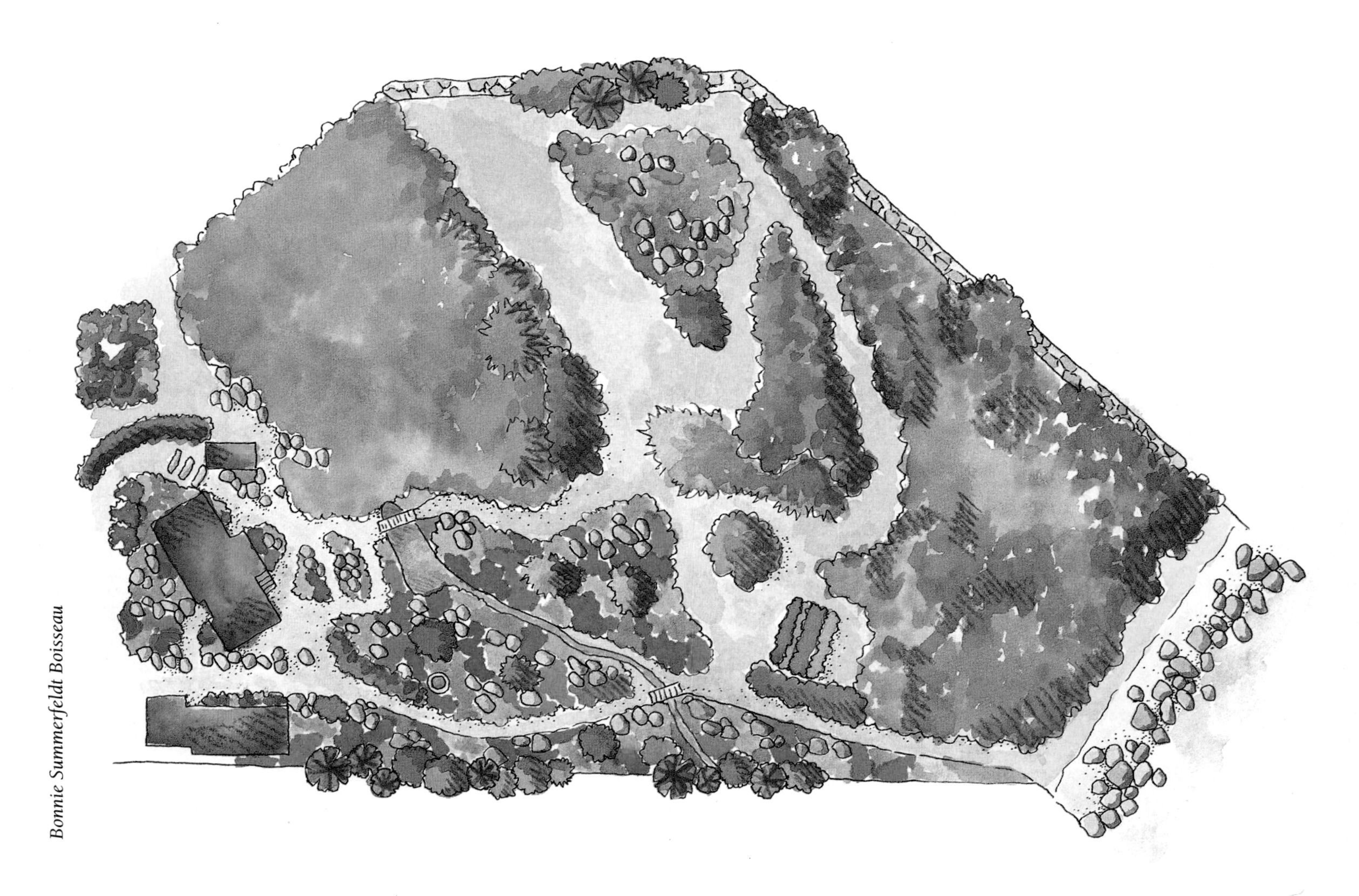

Bonnie Summerfeldt Boisseau

***Previous page:** A beautiful garden surrounds the Ostrom home.*

Right: Papaver burseri *grows in the drywall.*

trate and shrubby spireas from a nursery in Surrey, British Columbia. Saxifrages and drabas, including *Draba rigida imbrecata* ("It looks like a yellow afro haircut when it's in bloom," Walter says) are laced together with woolly thyme. The thyme tends to get out of hand and is weeded out annually. The face of the rock retaining wall is a showcase for more alpines. The white bells of *Campanula cochleariifolia alba* nod in the soft summer Atlantic breeze. This campanula spreads quickly, but it's fairly easy to control. Armeria hugs the wall like little green pincushions; its flowers look like large pink hatpins. Pale pink *Gypsophila repens rosea* cascades down the wall, too.

Walter grows many of his alpines from seed he obtains as a member of the Alpine Garden Club of British Columbia. "The only way to get many of these slow-growing plants is to grow them from seed yourself. Nurseries don't have the time to grow them, and wouldn't profit from doing so," Walter says.

Native plants are also included in this bed, hinting at Walter's understanding of what grows best in his demanding climate. One noteworthy example, not widely cultivated, is *Empetrum eamesii*, known locally as rockberry. Its narrow-leaved branches hug the dry stone wall, and the plants are covered with pink to red berries in the fall.

alter Ostrom's lath house is a homemade structure with myriad uses, particularly in his garden's windy location on the coast of Nova Scotia. The lack of shade trees allows hot summer sun to shine unrelentingly on young plants and seedlings, and Walter says the lath house saves many from death by desiccation.

The shelter is approximately ten by thirteen feet (three by four metres) . The laths are 1.2 inches (three centimetres) wide, and are attached with gaps of an equal width between them, which allows fifty percent of the available sunlight through; the spacing also means that shadows and sunlight are never in one place too long.

The interior of the lath house is moist and woods-like, a microclimate where testy plants such as ferns thrive (he often starts them from spores) and rhododendrons can be started from seed. Walter uses pure, freshly ground spaghnum moss to start his rhododendron seedlings, and they often don't germinate for up to two months; the damp shade of the lath house provides ideal growing conditions and gives the new plants a chance to adapt to the coastal Nova Scotia climate.

Lath houses have many variations that can be adapted to the home garden. For example, a cold frame could be turned into a small lath house by placing laths over the glass top. Or green or black nylon shadecloth, available at nurseries, may be attached to any size structure to provide almost the same growing conditions as a lath house.

Once the studio was built and landscaped, Walter turned his attention to the rest of the property. He built up the thin soil, which varies from fine, peaty sand to mineral-rich clay, with compost and a custom-made mix of coarse peat, sand, bark and mushroom compost. "I've had several truckloads brought in over the years," Walter says. "I found regular purchased topsoil inadequate."

The Ostroms have two composting systems on the go. One houses garden and kitchen waste; the other is made up of leaves Walter collects

by asking residents of nearby Halifax for their curb-side bags in the fall. Oak leaves are especially coveted because they make fine, rich compost. Walter relies on compost not only as a soil-enricher, but as an annual mulch to help keep weeds down.

While he worked on enriching the soil, Walter considered ways to tame the strong south winds he was warned about. He knew he needed to shelter his exposed site if he planned to alter the landscape at all. First, he planted three hundred Japanese black pine (*Pinus thunbergiana*) to shelter the garden from the winds. Only twenty-five survived, but they turned out to be particularly hardy stock, freely producing seed. But the south winds, which are predominantly wet and warm, weren't a problem after all; it was the overland wind from the northwest that did the most damage. "Unfortunately, it took me eight years to realize this," Walter says.

By this time Walter made another discovery. He noticed that no matter how cold the winter, there were always bits of native shrubbery growing between the rocks, sheltered from the wind. He began to look at these hardy natives with new respect and started a search for cultivated relatives, predicting they would also survive in his garden. One of his favourite native plants is the lovely low-growing *Kalmia poliifolia*, a sub-shrub with tiny clusters of bright rose-pink flowers in spring. It's a member of the Ericaceae family, of which rhododendrons are also members. Intrigued, Walter began planting various hardy species of rhododendrons, with glorious results. Particularly successful is *Rhododendron carolinianum*, native to the slopes of North Carolina's Blue Ridge

Above: *Walter grows his rhododendron seedlings in this home-built lath house.*

Mountains, with its pale-rose to purple flowers. Another native from the same region is *R. vaseyi*, with rose blossoms spotted brown. The white form *R. v. album* has pink flower buds for up to three weeks before they open to pure white. Some Asian species of rhododendron are also hardy in Ostrom's garden. *R. schlippenbachii* is deciduous but its leaves turn a rich bronze in fall. Large pale pink blooms that appear on the naked stems in the spring make the shrub look like an Oriental brush painting. For fragrance, Walter grows *R. impeditum*, which forms dense, low mounds covered with mauve to purplish-blue flowers. Walter grows all his rhododendrons from seed.

Always on the lookout for more hardy plants, Walter found low-growing conifers not only thrived in his garden, but provided a wonderful soft green to accent the many rock outcroppings. The new growth on Serbian spruce (*Picea omorika nana*) echoes the chartreuse flowers of nearby *Euphorbia polychroma*, while ground-hugging Korean spruce (*Abies koreana*) softens the rocks' hard edges. Several cultivars of *Juniperus horizontalis*, including 'Bar Harbour' and 'Blue Rug', cast bluish-grey shadows among the spiky, glaucous foliage of dianthus, which grows everywhere. The dozens of varieties—many are gifts from friends—seem to revel in the rock crevices.

"Once I recognized the endless possibilities of suitable native plants," says Walter, "I knew I could work up the landscape and create a natural-looking garden that would also be easy to maintain."

Left: *High-altitude rhododendrons and other alpines grow snugly between the rocks.*

Right: *Walter's studio nestles between the sea and his beautiful garden.*

The Neighbourly Gardens

of Doreen and Laurie Freeman & Patrick and Mary Spence-Thomas

Photographs by Bert Klassen

n Cabbagetown, a wonderfully preserved hundred-year-old piece of downtown Toronto, rows of beautifully restored Victorian-style homes hide myriad backyard retreats, small garden jewels so close to each other that they demand a neighbourhood camaraderie. These two, tucked behind a pair of tiny, attached brick houses and owned by two professional couples, are no exception. Each one fits neatly into its narrow ten- by forty-foot (three- by twelve-metre) space, and utilizes every bit of it.

Above: *The Spence-Thomas waterfall cleverly reuses an old water pump.*

Despite their proximity, the gardens are very different. Patrick and Mary Spence-Thomas's is very Canadian, utilizing cedar decking and natural materials everywhere, including the small pond and waterfall. Doreen and Laurie Freeman's garden embodies the English style, with pastel perennials, brick pavers and light-coloured wood backgrounds.

But it's the garages that are the focal points of both gardens. Both are so cleverly hidden behind fanciful rear façades (the business ends look like ordinary garages and face the laneway behind the houses) that one would never guess they house the families' cars plus garbage pails and sundry items. Both pairs of owners collaborated on the construction of the garages but decided to finish them differently, to carry out the themes of their own gardens.

The Freemans wanted a Victorian façade and chose a misty-grey painted clapboard with white trim. A beautiful stained-glass window and an iron fretwork railing finish off the doorway. Both were found during the Freemans' frequent visits to antique and secondhand shops. "We were told

Bonnie Summerfeldt Boisseau

the fretwork was once a bracket holding a shelf in place," says Doreen.

Both Doreen and Laurie love old-fashioned cottage-style flowers, and from the beginning Doreen wanted to have a garden like those she remembers from her childhood in England. She and Laurie sketched out a plan that's all pathway and flower beds—in addition to the small patio at the rear of the house. The wide beds are bisected by sinuously curving paths, and a lovely old bench was set against the wood fence halfway down the garden, where it catches the late-afternoon sun. "Our soil wasn't great five years ago when we started, but over time we've added manure, compost and peat to improve it," Doreen says. "Because of our limited space we don't compost, but we scrounge it from our neighbours."

Previous page: *These two completely different gardens create a restful oasis in the heart of Metropolitan Toronto.*

The colour scheme is shades of blue, pink, and lavender to deep purple, and the beds contain favourite flowers: columbines, irises, delphiniums, roses and clematis, and a little pink rock cress (*Arabis alpina rosea*) grown from seed purchased at Victoria's Butchart Gardens. "We take pleasure in every flower," says Doreen. "And there's always something blooming, from the deep purple, almost black tulips in spring to the pinkish bracts of the *Hydrangea paniculata* and those dear little pink roses, which often bloom into November."

Container plants are a feature of the garden, and include a wonderful old chimney pot planted every year with trailing variegated English ivy and the sun-tolerant New Guinea impatiens, whose dark foliage and pink flowers blend just right with the colours of the perennial border. One planter contains a corkscrew hazel (*Corylus avellana* 'Contorta'). "It used to be in the border, but it looked so ugly during the summer covered with twisted green leaves we put it in a pot and grow morning glories through it now," says Doreen. "But the twisted branches add something to the garden in winter."

Over the fence, which provides privacy when the couples want it but is just the right height for a neighbourly chat, lies the garden of Patrick and Mary Spence-Thomas. Just like the Canadian landscape, it's designed around wood, water and rocks, and the façade of the garage is reminiscent of the porch on a pioneer cottage, complete with rocking chair. Bold stone steps take the visitor from the porch to the wooden decking and raised flower beds. The pond and waterfall take up most of one side of the path, and, as in the Freemans' garden, there's a bench placed to catch the late-day sun. A handsome wooden pergola juts out from the back of the house. It's alive with hanging baskets of impatiens and a tumbling mass of silver lace vine (*Polygonum aubertii*). Mary had admired the plant on a neighbour's house, so she videotaped it—a handy way to remember what plants look like—then knocked on the neighbour's door to ask what it was called.

Above: *Patrick and Mary's rustic garage façade suggests an old country cabin.*

The winter before they dug their garden the Spence-Thomases pored over garden books for ideas. Because of their dog, they needed hard, undiggable surfaces and planting beds as dog-proof as possible. Using their computer, they devised variations of a basic plan and took them to a landscaping firm. The firm thought their plans were "cute" and quoted an incredible sum to implement them. So Mary enlisted the aid of her brother Franc, and she and Patrick worked along with him to build structural parts of the garden.

The initial work included burying conduit to carry service wires. "The space is so small we didn't want any unsightly overhead wires," says Patrick. They also put down grey industrial vinyl as a pond liner before they installed the wooden decking, which hides the edge of the pond. "Rocks and plants hide the rest of the nasty bits," says Patrick. He worked out on the computer the sizes of the rocks required, and many of them were brought back by family and friends from vacations.

Once the basic structure and the beds were in place, they were topped up with a rich blend of soil from a garden supply store. "Of course,

he eye-catching garage façades are the features of the Freeman and Spence-Thomas gardens, but a closer look reveals how the plants chosen by each couple further reflects their taste and carries through their gardens' colour schemes.

In the Spence-Thomas garden a lot of green has been used to great advantage to cut down on maintenance. The soft, needle-like foliage of low and upright junipers (all three cultivars of *Juniperus chinensis*) lead the eye to the next level where weeping *Caragana arborescens pendula*, with its pea-like foliage, adds a striking textural feature. The cedar garage façade is draped with wisteria; below it the bold rocks of the water feature are softened by the graceful foliage of a Japanese maple.

In the Freemans' garden next door, grey, silver and bluish plants work as a perfect background for the pink and blue cottage-garden plants. On the fence a fine form of variegated *Euonymus fortunei* gives year-round texture. Lower down, hugging the ground, silver-leaved *Lamium maculatum* scrambles under the blue-green palmate foliage of a large clump of monkshood (*Aconitum napellus*). Nearby, in the shade, grows a bold clump of *Hosta fortunei*. The same types of foliage are mirrored on the sunny side of the garden where more silver lamium grows as a soft bed for the sword-like foliage of *Iris germanica*. Even in the absence of flowers, there is always a pleasing scene.

we fertilize with manure and compost on an annual basis," Mary says. "We've been composting for the past four years. We generally put it on the garden in the spring, but this past season we decided to experiment and dig it in before winter. Patrick uses a riddle made for him by a friend to sieve out the chunky bits, but each year there are fewer and fewer of them. That's probably because we're chopping up the material very small."

The basic structure of Mary's and Patrick's garden includes many small evergreens: various junipers, bird's-nest spruce (*Picea abies* 'Nidiformis') and a Montgomery dwarf blue spruce (*Picea pungens* 'Montgomery'). But Mary's favourite tree is a cutleaf Japanese maple (*Acer palmatum*) bought with fifty loonies given to her by Franc to spend on the garden.

She named the tree Franc. "We want our garden to be filled with friends with names," says Mary. She positioned the evergreens before planting them, carefully putting shapes and textures together to frame the view of the garden from inside the house during all the seasons. Other climbers, in addition to the silver lace vine, play a role in the small garden: a wisteria scrambles over the garage porch and a climbing hydrangea (*Hydrangea anomala*) clings to the fence between the gardens.

The couple's computer acts as their garden diary: all of the plants are recorded, and the list is getting long. "We may have started with a construction plan, but we have no planting plan. I call my method flukus maximus," laughs Mary. "We've blown a lot of bread on plants."

Each summer Mary plants many annuals, including bright-coloured impatiens and coleus. As the shrubs get larger, providing less light and space, her annual choices change. She's also using soft feature plants between the shrubs and annuals; a favourite is *Artemisia schmidtiana* 'Silver Mound', whose soft, fluffy silver leaves sparkle with moisture after a summer shower.

Above: *The Freemans' cool English cottage garden.*

Left: *The pale, delicate blossoms of a tree fuchsia are complemented by the ornate planter.*

Mary and Patrick love their garden. "Because we lead busy lives and have limited time, our concentration has been on minimum maintenance/maximum pleasure," says Mary. "I'm still a beginner, and I find gardening a challenge. You need patience: you plant, you wait, observe things as they grow, you enjoy some things and change others. Gardening slows us down, causes us to reflect and returns us to our roots, so to speak."

Next door, Doreen and Laurie feel much the same way. "Gardening quiets the restless soul," Doreen says, "We look on ours as an oasis in the middle of our busy lives."

Right: *An inviting, cool path made from aggregate stepping-stones is lined with* Campanula rotundifolia.

dug in sheep manure, compost, oak leaves and bone meal. I garden organically, and it's important to me not to poison my patch of earth."

At the front of the house, where the lawn rose in a small hump to meet the floor of the verandah, they created a three-tiered rock garden; it's now the home of some of Lisa's favourite alpine plants interplanted with more perennials. But during their first winter in the house, before all the heavy groundwork began, Lisa's watchful eye had been recording the daily path of the sun through the garden, noting sunny and shady areas so she could determine what plants should be planted where. This is especially important in a heavily treed garden like Lisa's—it's important to match

isa Preston's artistic eye and her talent for ferreting out inexpensive materials to make garden accessories is illustrated well in the simple but effective rose arbour at the side of her house. Lisa had always wanted a light, airy-looking arbour of copper that would age to a verdigris finish often seen in illustrations of old European gardens, but was unable to find just what she wanted. Then inspiration struck: why not use plumber's copper piping?

At a local plumbing supply company she found just the piping she wanted, and laid out various lengths in the aisle to create a gothic arch for her arbour. To join the lengths and create the angles she chose from the joints and connections readily available in the bins on the shelves. The sales clerk approached to see if she needed help, and, seeing her arrangement on the floor, he asked if she was an artist. "No," she smiled, "I'm just a gardener."

Once she had the pieces home, Lisa pushed the support pipes eighteen inches (forty-five centimetres) into the ground and assembled the arch, using two-part epoxy glue to seal the joints. It's been standing for over four years now, an attractive and original accessory in the garden.

plants to the environment, and just as important to experiment, to move plants around. "My plants should have frequent-flier points for the miles they've put in on the wheelbarrow," laughs Lisa. "My garden is never static. I acknowledge my plants' individual requirements, but then I move them to suit the design of the garden. First and foremost, I choose sculptured

Above: *The shady back garden.*

plants because flowers seldom last. The texture, shape and colour of leaves is important. And placement is everything. I mean, how pleasing would it be to plant all the spiky plants together? A garden needs harmony." As if to prove her point, a harmonious arrangement hoves into view: a cushion of pale pink tuberous begonias next to several clumps of soft pink and white impatiens, set off by the bold leaves of *Bergenia schmidtii* and the feathery shapes of *Astilbe japonica* and arching ferns.

Harmony in planting is not everything, of course. A garden needs shape and structure as well. The paths of Lisa's garden are its bones. They lead to all its secret areas. Made of square, mixed-aggregate blocks in pleasant earth tones, the paths fade into the background among the exuberant plants in high summer, but are visible enough that one doesn't trample on favourite plants. The fence that runs along the back of the lot, in front of the maples, and up the south side of the garden, is a subtle barrier—it's made of chainlink, usually an ugly material, but it's black, and seems to disappear even in winter. In summer it's clothed in vines, roses and a couple of native plants: the wild grape (*Vitis riparia*) and bittersweet (*Celastrus scandens*).

"Gardening should be fun," Lisa says, and her own sense of whimsy surfaces everywhere in her garden. She frequents garage sales for objects to use—the pudgy Buddha, for example, happily ensconced under a cedar bough and surrounded by daylily foliage. When Lisa found him he was bright red and sadly broken, but she glued him together, painted him black and gave him a new place in life. Then there are the three jolly frogs holding hands and gazing skyward with their mouths agape, apparently croaking with delight at being in Lisa's garden. But it is the pair of legs appearing to dive into the pond that stops you in your tracks. The remains of a store mannequin, Lisa put them there before a summer dinner party, and they were such a conversation piece they stayed. "Sometimes I add flippers for extra effect," Lisa says.

The pond was no easy undertaking. Lisa and Richard dug an oval hole five feet by twenty inches (1.5 metres by 50 centimetres deep)—the depth required to grow water lilies successfully—added a thick layer of newspapers, and lined it with chloride sheeting. The edges are hidden with grey slate paving stones, many of which are partially covered by abundant greenery. A small stone face hides under the branches of a spruce tree next to the pond and spouts water from its mouth into a beautiful brass dish. A potted *Zebrina pendula* with gorgeous plum and silver foliage sets off the vignette to perfection. And, of course, the sound of water adds to the peace of the garden and attracts birds.

Lisa keeps her garden safe during Winnipeg's harsh winters by mulching heavily with leaves. She piles them about a foot (thirty centimetres) deep. "I leave the tops on the perennials so I can easily find them in spring," she says. "Then I compost the mulch." To keep the many bulbs in the garden blooming for a longer time, she leaves the mulch in place on some of them, uncovering a few every week or so. The ground stays cooler and keeps them from flowering all at once.

Why does Lisa garden? "Because it feeds my soul," she says. She walks and talks gardens —in fact, since this one has become established she's taken on a few garden design contracts in Winnipeg and Vancouver. "My work and my life are now one."

* * *

Many of the stones and rocks in Lisa Preston's garden look as if they've been there since the house was built at the turn of the century. In fact Lisa creates their old, moss-covered appearance in a few months. She gathers some moss from a nearby lake, pops it in a blender with a bit of sheep manure and some water, blends it to a paste and paints it right onto the rocks. Before you know it a green coating is taking root.

Of course, Lisa suggests using an old blender for this.

Above: *Attractive fungi and a smiling Buddha's head enhance a cool corner of the garden.*

Right: *Lisa uses found objects, such as this urn, to accent her garden.*

The Zen Garden

of Rosemary Pauer

Photographs by Bert Klassen

hen Rosemary Pauer and her family moved to their semi-detached house in Bramalea, north and east of Toronto, the back garden contained nothing at all. In the front there was a meagre foundation planting of four upright junipers plus a patch of turf laid by the developers—and it was fast turning brown because of the strong sun of the southern exposure and a lack of water.

To approach the house today, several years later, is to know a dedicated gardener lives there. The foundation planting still contains the four junipers, now trimmed bonsai fashion and hinting at the Oriental mood of the garden behind the house, but the dry brown lawn is long gone, replaced by a mass of flowers—among them pink and white yarrow (*Achillea millefolium*), coral bells (*Heuchera sanguinea*), Oriental poppies and several species of penstemon. It's a tapestry of colour, with everything happily growing into and between one another, and all woven together by soft grey lamb's ears (*Stachys byzantina*). "I grow everything in this bed from seed," Rosemary says with a touch of deserved pride. "And every plant must be drought tolerant, because I never water this area."

Above: *A snow lantern is a focal point of the small pond.*

Rosemary's back garden started with a few trees planted for privacy and to attract birds. It has evolved into a lush, Japanese-style retreat filled with inviting rocks and crannies. The Japanese mood was inspired by a book Rosemary's family gave her a few years ago: *The Art of Zen Gardens*. Although she'd been gardening successfully for years, she felt her approach was haphazard. The book gave her a sense of direction. "The Zen philosophy allowed me to garden from the heart, and for the feel of the place," Rosemary says. "It gave me a purpose."

Bonnie Summerfeldt Boisseau

Previous page: *An overview of Rosemary's small green world.*

But the physical work of creating the garden hasn't been easy. The soil was uncompromising heavy yellow clay, wet and slippery in the winter and like concrete in the summer. Soil amendments were necessary to grow anything at all, so Rosemary has become an expert compost-maker. "My poor family," Rosemary laughs. "I drag them out into the country every fall to collect leaves—about forty bags each year." Some leaves are used as a winter mulch (over the following seasons they rot and add humus to the soil), but most are added to the compost bins over the year. The back garden, entered through a vine-clad arch, is like a miniature rainforest. There are many shades of green, from chartreuse and emerald to olive, balanced by the rich plum foliage of several Japanese maples. In the oppressive humidity of a typical Ontario summer, the scene is cooling and calming. "People tell me that coming into my garden is like entering a different world," says Rosemary.

Above: ***Rosemary's garden expresses her interest in the philosophy of Zen. Peonies*** (Paeonia lactiflora), *Siberian iris* (Iris sibirica), *and hostas backed by a red Japanese maple* (Acer japonicum) *create a picture of serenity.*

The abundant green of the garden makes the flowers stand out. One's eye is immediately drawn to a bamboo arbour at the rear of the garden covered with vivid blue morning glories (*Ipomoea tricolor* 'Heavenly Blue'). Enormous clumps of single peonies, including Rosemary's favourite white, 'Jan van Leeuwan', and several tree peonies (*Paeonia suffruticosa*) are perfectly placed. "I coaxed these along," says Rosemary. "They were cheapies in cardboard boxes I got from a garden centre."

The garden is enclosed by cedar hedging interspersed with fences clad with Virginia creeper (*Parthenocissus quinquefolia*). The tiny space is crammed full of so many vignettes one can't possibly see them all at once. Stepping-stone paths lead to various focal points: a tiny pool with a Japanese snow lantern at its edge; a dark brown, glazed earthenware pot; a *tsukubai* created by Rosemary from cement and peat moss moulded in a plastic bag. Some stepping stones are set in loose gravel, suggesting stream beds; others grow in patches of grass and moss. The path that leads to the pool is framed by the overhanging branches of a honey locust (*Gleditsia triacanthos*), with its light, airy compound leaves; below the locust a gorgeous plum-foliaged Japanese maple (*Acer japonicum atropurpureum*) acts as understorey, and lower still *Hosta fortunei aurea* and *H. f.* 'marginato-alba' make bold statements accented by the staccato foliage of *Iris sibirica caerulea*. Ferns, astilbe and Japanese blood grass (*Imperata cylindrica rubra*) behind the pool complete the tranquil picture.

The brown earthenware pot is set in another scene. It's surrounded by

osemary Pauer is sometimes called the connoisseur of compost by her gardening friends—she has the whole process down to an art. She says it's important to have two compost bins at work at the same time—one actively "cooking" the ingredients, as she describes it, while the other is ready for use. Her compost bins are made from six-foot (two-metre) lengths of eight- by eight-inch (twenty- by twenty-centimetre) lumber. Rosemary cuts them in half and builds the bin in a rustic style. No nails are needed because the lumber is heavy enough to stay put as it is laid—alternately at right angles one on top of the other, leaving equal gaps between each one for good air circulation. This makes the bins easy to dismantle when the compost is ready.

In addition Rosemary has two purchased plastic bins she uses in winter for kitchen scraps. All the bins are screened from the street and the neighbours by vine-covered trellises. This type of structure can help eliminate the bad name composting often receives in urban areas.

Rosemary plants mint all around the compost bins because it smells good every time it's bruised by walking on it. Comfrey grows happily between the bins, providing a constant supply of leaves for the compost.

Composting is a vital part of every successful garden and utilizing the composting space as Rosemary does makes it far more appealing.

Achillea ptarmica 'The Pearl' and placed under the feathery foliage of two trees native to Ontario: a white pine (*Pinus strobus*), pruned back annually in the Japanese way, by reducing the length of the new shoots while they are still green; and a slender tamarack (*Larix laricina*), a deciduous tree that brightens each fall with fine golden foliage. Behind the trees grow hardy shrub roses—a white 'Henry Hudson' and a pink 'Jens Munk'.

Birds are much in evidence in Rosemary's garden. "At first there were none at all, but as the garden grew and the neighbours put in maples and other trees, the birds started to come," Rosemary says. "Then I started to plant shrubs and plants that provide food and shelter. That brought more. And of course there's the water, which is available to them year-round. I don't use any sprays or chemicals, so the garden is full of insects, plus worms, cats and squirrels. A raccoon visits at night—but he's not especially welcome."

Like most gardeners, Rosemary has several favourite plants, not just one: Japanese maples, for their beautiful foliage and delicate shape in the winter ("I have seven right now"); ferns, especially the Japanese painted fern (*Athyrium goeringianum*), which tolerates sun; and clematis, especially the species ("which I grow from seed from the Ontario Rock Garden Society"). She lets the clematis scramble through bushes and trees as well as up the trellises. She also likes astilbe, especially the white foamy ones, and hostas, of course, because they're so lush and luxurious and do well anywhere.

Rosemary is a down-to-earth gardener who admits she's not interested in rare or difficult plants. "It's the overall peace and quiet I am aiming for," she says. "I want my garden to look good in winter, so I have many evergreens and the snow viewing lantern to look at, and the birds who visit. We even get the occasional hawk, who will swoop down to take a bird from the feeder.

"My garden has taught me so much—about growth, life, death and renewal. Nothing lasts forever, but nothing is wasted. It's all turned into something else."

***Left:** A tranquil scene is created by the soft overhead textures of honey locust* (Gleditsia triacnathos) *and Japanese maple balanced by an underplanting of bold hosta leaves.*

***Far left:** Moss adds to the ancient feeling of Rosemary's homemade* tsukubai.

The Impressionist Garden

of Henriette & Guy Miral

pproaching Henriette and Guy Miral's garden in St. Lazar, Quebec, is nearly half the fun: as you get closer to the house, patches of colour fill the horizon like an Impressionist painting and are mirrored in the smooth surface of a large, natural pond. Swaths of ornamental grass sway in a light breeze and in the distance horses graze in a green pasture. It's a scene of pastoral peace.

Meeting the energetic, outgoing couple behind the enormous garden (it covers three acres/1.2 hectares of the property's thirty acres/12 hectares and is, in Henriette's words, "too little") is the other half of the equation. Here is the perfect pair, the symbiotic relationship: Henriette obsessed with making the perfect garden, Guy obsessed with the machinery to accomplish the task. "I call them my Tonkas," he says, showing off a tractor with a front-end shovel, another with a rototiller, the bulldozer—which helped him do much of the early work in the five-year-old garden—and the two hand-held rototillers. Naturally, one also needs a lawn trimmer, and the mechanical compost grinder may be the most important tool of all.

Photographs by Canapress/Allen McInnis

***Above:** The lily (*Lilium *'Stargazer') scents the summer evening air.*

But tools can't begin to take the place of inspiration, of the artist's approach to planning and design, and for this Guy gives Henriette full credit. "My wife is a machine herself," he says with a laugh. A practising physician, she's up with the sun and works in the garden till after darkness falls. In it grow one thousand varieties of plants, mostly hardy perennials.

This garden is the couple's second. "The first had a couple of cottage-style beds filled with every possible colour," says Henriette. "But that was

Previous page: *Reflected in the lake is a replica of Monet's bridge and the island with its gazebo, a result of Guy's hard work.*

before my accident." The accident is not to be brushed off lightly: Henriette's horse fell on her—after Henriette had fallen off the horse—and Henriette spent months in bed recuperating. A friend brought her a series of colour plates of Monet's garden at Giverny, France, and she was entranced. It was exactly what she wanted in a new garden—something more serene, with masses of colour the eye could rest on. As Henriette lay in bed she envisioned a lake with an island, extensive and harmonious flower beds, a gazebo and a small mountain on the horizon.

Once she had recuperated, Guy says there was no stopping her. She pointed and Guy manned the machinery, creating the lake here and the island there, a small mountain at the end of the lake and a small arching bridge copied from Monet's.

Once the construction was done (although "done" isn't an acceptable word to the Mirals: Guy added the planned summer house in the summer of '93 and there is, no doubt, more to come) it was time to amend the heavy clay soil. At least the material was at hand: with the horses there is a constant supply of well-rotted manure, the envy of all good gardeners. Copious amounts of peat moss were also added to the planting areas. For maintenance, compost is added annually and small amounts of manure when it's needed. "The earth is good now," says Henriette. "Your hands just slip into it."

The large perennial garden nearest the house was one of the first areas to be planted. Perennials do well in this part of Quebec—they thrive in the clay soil and stay cozy under a dependable winter blanket of snow. But like most beds, it took time to get it established. Rabbits and field mice were a particular problem—they seemed to eat the new plants as soon as Henriette put them in the ground. Now that the border is well established and flowing harmoniously, as the creator saw it in her dreams, rodents bother the garden less, but because of the rural location there will always be some damage.

Below: *Monet would surely approve of Henriette and Guy's beautiful garden.*

Astilbes in white to pale pinks and darker rose are perhaps Henriette's favourite plant. She likes them because they resist the cold and ask only for sufficient water. And of course they bloom thickly, their feathery wands massed together. Massing is the key to this beautiful border: it's a great drift of colour, not patches of a few plants of each kind. More pink and silver is provided by old-fashioned *Sedum spectabile*, with its succulent foliage and dense, flat umbels of rose-pink flowers late in the summer; the plants also attract butterflies and bees, which buzz around them in late summer. The lupins seed freely and are continuously introducing new colour hybrids to the garden. Drifts of gorgeous blue delphiniums and masses of bee balm (*Monarda didyma*), also known as bergamot, add to the colour. Henriette particularly likes the red bee balm because it

While Henriette Miral lay recovering from a broken leg, she dreamed about a new garden to be made up of naturalized swaths of colour and lots of diversity in shapes and texture. Once the leg was healed, she took a practical approach and created a five-year plan for its completion. Some of it has come about faster than planned because, like many gardeners, Henriette and her husband, Guy, tend to be obsessed with their avocation.

But in their speed they didn't cut corners. They followed Henriette's well-thought-out design, which was planned so the garden could be viewed from the living room at all times of the year. They chose trees, shrubs and rocks whose shapes could be enjoyed even in the depths of winter. Henriette's advice is to implement your garden plan one step at a time—starting with the main point of view from the living room. Plan the bones of the entire garden, its overall structure and main points of interest (in the Mirals' garden, the gazebo and the replica of Monet's curved bridge at Giverny), even if they aren't put into place immediately.

The first area Henriette planted was the perennial garden, which has been added to in profusion over the years. Perennial plants and bulbs can always be moved, but it's not as easy with trees and shrubs, and nearly impossible with structures like bridges.

encourages the visits of hummingbirds and adds a pleasant honey-lemon scent to the air. More scent is provided by many cultivars of *Phlox paniculata*; their large panicles of pale pink blossoms perfume the evening air in high summer. Yellow is provided by *Heliopsis helianthoides*. All these forms are derived from plants native to southern Ontario, Quebec, and parts of New York State.

Henriette has a special appreciation of native plants—angelica, for instance, with its magnificent chartreuse umbels a foot (thirty centimetres) in diameter borne on stems almost three feet (one metre) tall. Cow parsley (*Heracleum sphondylium*) is another plant with a giant umbel; its blossoms are white. Stands of beautiful goldenrod, which gets so much undeserved bad publicity at hay-fever time (it seldom causes an allergic reaction because its pollen is too heavy to be windborne) have been incorporated in the border, along with many ornamental grasses.

Behind the border is the barn, a wonderful structure that adds to the sylvan setting. Guy made the large, natural-looking pond and its island, where the new summer house is located; from it the garden can be viewed. Access to the island is over an exact replica of Monet's bridge, its perfect arch reflected in the dark water.

There are different themes among the twenty beds that flow from behind the renovated farmhouse to the southern bank of the lake. On a small hill just behind a great mass of astilbes Henriette has made a small meditation garden. Instead of a mass of colour, it is a restful blend of greens, with a bit of gold and blue provided by junipers, and a carefully placed rock.

In the distance, on the gentle rise behind the lake, is the rose garden. Henriette acknowledges it seems strange to plant a rose garden so far from the house, but it was planned to give visitors a destination on their strolls through the property. She also grows the legendary blue Himalayan poppy (*Meconopsis betonicifolia*), two hundred cultivars and species of iris, two hundred rose bushes (many are 'Bonica' types, which are hardier here—an advantage to a gardener who has already lost some three hundred roses to winter kill), and thirty kinds of lilac, whose heady perfume fills the air in early summer.

Henriette's goal in her redesigned garden was a sense of fullness, richness and profusion, which she's achieved with dedication and hours of work. "I even weed in the dark," she says, hastening to add that like most gardeners she doesn't consider it work and she doesn't know when to stop. This applies to the garden, too. "It's difficult not to expand when you have no natural barriers to stop you," she says. "I'm always creating new limits."

Left: *An old Quebec wooden barn makes a wonderful background for the perennial border.*

Far left: *Henriette's interpretation of an Impressionist's garden.*

The Bloom Garden

of Audrey Burrows

Photographs by Brian Harder

efore Audrey and John Burrows moved to Calgary from Brampton, Ontario, some ten years ago, friends warned them the climate in the foothills was so difficult they'd probably have to give up gardening. "That was a challenge," says Audrey. "What serious gardener could fail to rise to it?"

Their exquisite, bloom-filled garden, as lovely as any you'd find in England (the couple's home country), has evolved in the usual trial—and error—fashion. "We were the first people in this new subdivision, and I didn't mind inheriting poor soil left by the developer's bulldozers," says John. "In every garden we've had since coming to Canada, I've had to dig up turf to make way for gardens. This one gave me a chance to plan from scratch."

Above: *The curved edging along Audrey's abundant mixed perennial bed allows the mower to run on it, thus eliminating the work of edging;* Gaillardia x grandiflora *forms a bold splash of colour in the foreground.*

The back of the pie-shaped lot, where the bulk of the garden grows, faces west and looks across the open prairie, with a view of the snow-capped Rocky Mountains in the distance. John designed the garden in a classical, yet flowing pattern: a wide perennial border traverses most of the lot; it's fronted by a gravel path and a central lawn. Originally the lot sloped gently upward toward the rear; John had it levelled off to accommodate the lawn and put in a rock garden instead of a retaining wall to support the soil. The rock garden is strategically placed near the deck at the back of the house and serves as a visual as well as a physical transition: it leads one's eye to the rest of the flowery scene.

Against the fence and soaking up the sun's rays on the northeast side of the lot are the raised vegetable garden, a homemade greenhouse and a cold frame, reached by shallow steps and a fine crazy-paving pathway.

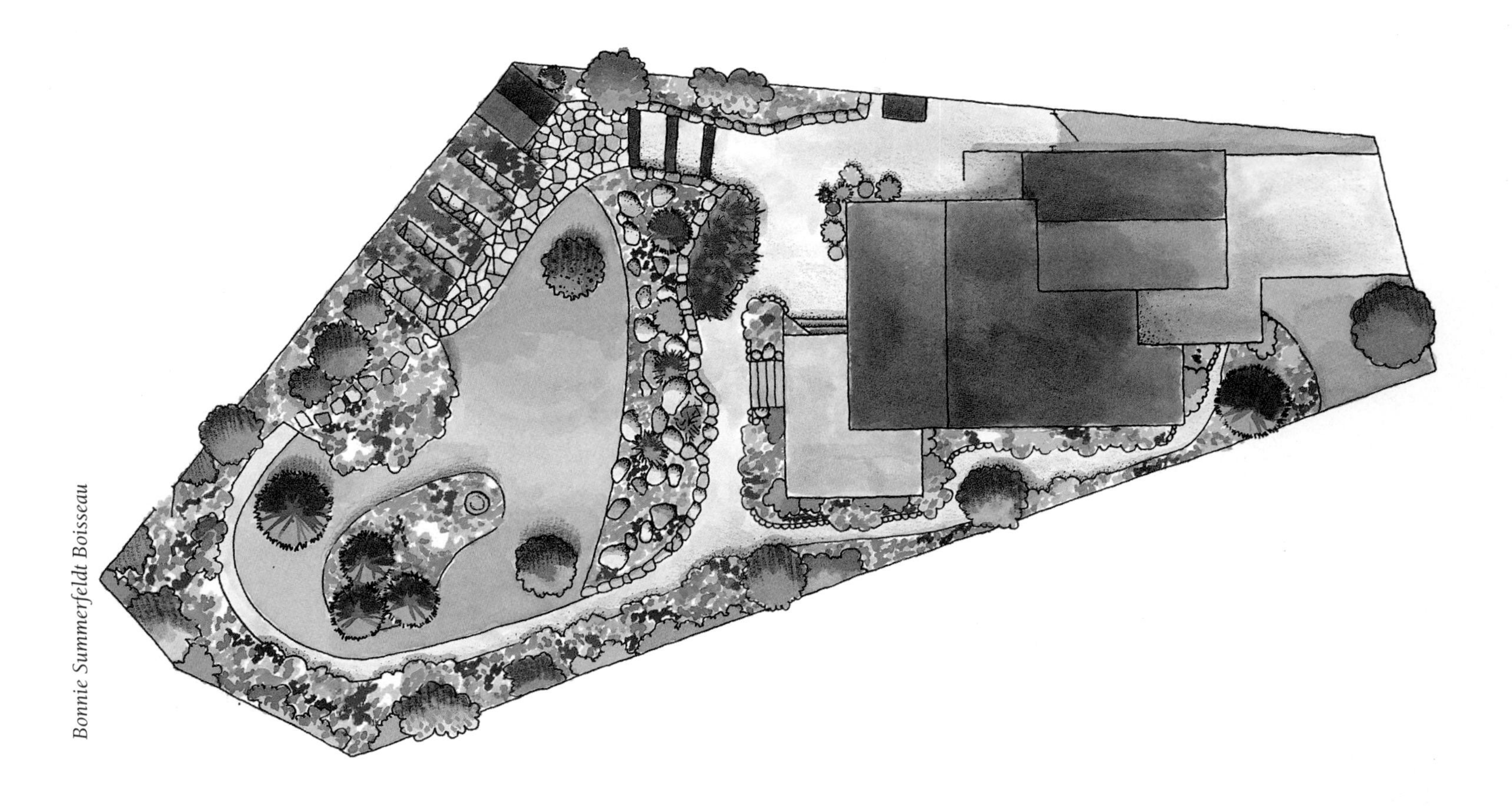
Bonnie Summerfeldt Boisseau

***Previous page:** The alpine area is in the foreground of this view from the house.*

John made the path from broken pieces of precast concrete left around the subdivision by the builders. He did most of the structural work in the garden himself, and says proudly that laying out the garden the first year—including several loads of topsoil—cost less than a hundred dollars.

The Burrows are indeed frugal gardeners who learn by doing. When they moved from Brampton, Audrey brought her large collection of houseplants as well as rooted cuttings or divisions of her favourite garden perennials. "I wasn't sure how available they'd be in Calgary," she says. They moved into a temporary home the first year and the plants were heeled into the garden and mulched well for the winter. "With some trepidation we went looking for the plants in April," says John. "When we got down close, we could see them turning green under the ice. At that moment we both felt there was hope for our gardening prospects here."

They readily admit conditions are different in Calgary, which has only about a hundred frost-free days a year but the promise of a long summer filled with sunshine. And of course there are the chinooks, which can lift winter-deadened spirits but start a deadly freeze/thaw cycle that can kill plants. To quickly familiarize herself with the differences, Audrey joined the Calgary Horticultural Society, an active group with about seventeen hundred members. She learned about starting seeds early indoors and hardening plants off in a cold frame so they're ready to be moved into their beds at the start of the short season. The greenhouse soon became a necessity, and it is utilized fully to get plants going early. During April and May it's heated at night to protect the seedlings from frost, and some tender vegetables live there all summer—a peek through the door in August reveals masses of plump, juicy tomatoes and peppers.

Audrey also learned about raised beds from horticultural society members. "The soil warms up so much earlier in raised beds," she says. John made theirs with recycled boards; the narrow beds are separated by crazy-paving pathways.

In summer the rock garden vibrates with colour, but the deep blue gentian (*Gentiana aucalis*) is Audrey's favourite. "It's formed a large clump—it seems to love the alkaline clay soil of the region," she says. Knotweed (*Polygonum affine*), a low green mass covered with six-inch (fifteen-centimetre) stems topped with rose-pink flowers, and hens and chickens (*Sempervivum tectorum*), its succulent rosettes of leaves now and then rewarding the Burrows with foot-tall (thirty-centimetre-high) spikes of pink flowers resembling exploding fireworks, also do well in the rock garden. The intense blue flowers of carpet bugleweed (*Ajuga reptans*) complement the pinks of early summer. Audrey allows Shirley poppies to self-seed among the alpines, all of which grow among pieces of driftwood, sandstone rocks and gravel, giving the small garden the feeling of a high alpine scree.

Below: *Gladiolas are an old favourite in the summer garden.*

The massed colours of the perennial borders on the perimeter of the property are echoed in great abundance in the island beds. The beds are augmented with annuals to fill in and extend the season. The delphiniums (*Delphinium grandiflorum*) are among Audrey's favourites. "They thrive in the cool nights and bright summer days of Alberta," says Audrey. They also like the soil: the Burrows prepared it well in the early days, and each year a mulch of well-rotted compost is applied. The flower spikes often reach six or seven feet (about two metres), and several will be produced in each clump. After the initial spikes are finished, Audrey cuts the stems back to just below the bloom and a whole new batch of shorter—but just as colourful—flower spikes are produced, giving the plant a long flowering period. As

udrey Burrows's experience as a gardener in Ontario and Alberta has given her a keen eye for pinpointing microclimates. Her advice is to observe your garden for a year, making notes of sunny spots, where water stays on the ground for any length of time and where snow drifts and tends to stay in winter. A place with a dependable snow cover is great for tender perennials and one that collects water is good for moisture-loving plants such as astilbe. Of course, conditions are going to change over the years, as shrubs and trees grow, fences go up, and you improve the quality of the soil.

In all of southern Alberta, winters are variable because of the warming effect of the chinooks and the harsh, chilling winds, which lead to severe winter dehydration. Audrey advises watering the garden deeply as late in the year as possible before the frosts come, plus a thick mulch of compost over the permanent plantings. During winter, snow is shovelled onto the plants—the combination of snow and mulch helps to conserve much-needed moisture in the soil, and keeps plants at a fairly even temperature during the fluctuating weather conditions.

Audrey believes in trying all kinds of plants, even if garden books say they can't grow in her garden's conditions. She gives a plant she likes a three-year trial—even if it means replanting a new one three years in a row. If by then it doesn't survive, she moves on to other tempting plants.

the delphiniums finish, tansy (*Tanacetum vulgare*) shoots three feet (one metre) into the air, sporting parsley-like foliage topped by dense heads of bright yellow buttons. "They're lovely in the border and great for drying too," says Audrey. Next to the tansy is a big clump of shasta daisies (*Chrysanthemum* x *superbum*) mixed with purple coneflower (*Echinacea purpurea*). Tumbling about in cottage-garden style in front is a large clump of rose-coloured yarrow (*Achillea millefolium*) and purple gayfeathers (*Liatris spicata*).

Forgotten favourites our grandmothers once grew also find a place in Audrey's garden—dense bushes of godetia and satin flower (*Clarkia amoena*), ranging from pale pink to dark red, each dense clump of flower heads like little Victorian posies. White annual mallow (*Lavatera trimestris alba*) forms two-foot (sixty-centimetre) clumps covered with large blossoms all season long. Painted tongue or Persian carpet flower (*Salpiglossis sinuata*), a two-foot (sixty-centimetre) branching annual, has large tubular flowers in rich colours deeply veined in contrasting purple, yellow and crimson. All of these annuals combine with daylilies and great clumps of *Achillea ptarmica* 'The Pearl'.

The raised vegetable beds produce excellent root vegetables—carrots, onions and beets for the cold cellar, and parsnips, which are heavily mulched in late fall and survive in the ground over winter, ready for good eating in early spring. Cabbages and edible-pod peas also do well. A bed of asparagus not only provides tasty shoots for the dinner table but also creates a lovely, ferny foil for the sweet peas that grow around the greenhouse each summer.

Audrey and John are organic gardeners to the core—three compost bins constantly churn out much-needed humus. In addition they keep a plastic bin by the house for kitchen waste. "In winter," says Audrey, "plastic bags take over—we never throw anything biodegradable away." In addition to the annual mulch of compost, peat is added as a soil conditioner.

"We don't use chemical pesticides," says John. "We prefer to hand pick bugs and stay on top of bothersome weeds, like chickweed and thistles, by pulling them up as they appear. Luckily we're never bothered by slugs or mildew—I think it's because we use underground soaker hoses, so there's never a lot of water sitting around on the leaves." The hoses are drained before winter, and when the beds receive a thick mulch to take them through the season, the hoses are protected along with the plants.

Audrey and John Burrows may be secretly pleased that their glorious Calgary garden has proved the doubting Thomases in the east quite wrong, but they're too polite to say it. "How can you help having a successful garden when gardening is such a compulsion?" she asks.

Left: *Audrey tends her impatiens and other potted annuals daily.*

Far left: *Daisies* (Chrysanthemum x superbum), *tansy* (Tanacetum vulgare), Achillea millefolium *and* Liatris spicata *provide a permanent summer flower arrangement in Audrey's garden.*

The Serene Garden

of Wayne Renaud

Photographs by Christopher Dew

Wayne Renaud's tranquil garden in Mississauga, Ontario, is simplicity itself, yet it's an amalgam of styles. Its strong geometry and sense of peace suggest the Orient, its walled courtyard the Mediterranean, and the materials and lifestyle are purely North American.

Wayne, a landscape architect who teaches at the University of Guelph and runs a small business in home and garden design with his partner, Gordon Webber, is no stranger to Canada's wide-open spaces. He grew up on the Prairies and has spent much of his time studying and photographing Canada's tundra and marshlands. "I consider our wilderness areas our greatest natural gardens," he says, "and I hope I've managed to get something of their spirit into my small urban garden."

Above: *Siberian iris and trickling water cool the heat of a summer day.*

When he and Gordon bought the tiny property, what's now the front garden was a long, twenty-foot-wide (six-metre) driveway leading to an old coach house, which had been severed from the original house. First Wayne and Gordon renovated the coach house, adding a second floor with a Palladian-style centre window and a bank of French doors on the main floor that open onto a sunny patio. It's a charming house, both modern and classic in design, and it demanded a garden equally as appealing.

The second project was the new garage/gatehouse, which fronts onto the street and echoes, in miniature, some of the design elements of the coach house. The garage is joined to the tall fence that encloses the garden by a handsome gate. Just inside the gate is the pond, the centrepiece of the garden. Its long, narrow shape and square stone basin—which constantly trickles water, drowning out the sounds of the

Bonnie Summerfeldt Boisseau

Previous page: *Eastern redbud* (Cercis canadensis) *and wisteria* (Wisteria sinensis) *are early-blooming species.*

busy street nearby—reflects the symmetry of the structures and dominates the garden. "It *is* the garden," says Wayne, who designed it and built it with Gordon. "You can't be anywhere on the property or in most of the house without seeing it or hearing it." Beside the pond a straight blue-slate flagstone path is laid on a bed of limestone screenings. It leads to the patio, which runs the width of the house and is, like the path, based on a grid pattern that matches the spacing of the French windows.

The patio is an enchanting place to be on a warm summer evening, inhaling the perfume of wisteria or feeding the koi that live in the pond. Two benches provide seating: a comfortably large wooden one and another made of Credit Valley limestone—the ruins of an old stone wall found on the property. The fountain's pedestal is also made from limestone, and the square basin was carved by a local stonesmith from a large slab. Although it reflects the grid of the paving, the basin was placed at an angle so it could be better viewed from the patio.

In summer the pond is rich with water sounds, darting fish, and the green pads of hardy water lilies, including *Nymphaea chromatella*, which has bronzy green leaves and large canary-yellow blossoms with deep yellow stamens. Non-hardy lilies wintered over indoors are placed in the pond in spring. "We have a night-blooming cultivar called 'Sir Galahad', " says Wayne. "It's beautifully scented, and the flowers—which must be ten inches (twenty-five centimetres) across—rise high above the water on a humid night." By midsummer the water temperature can exceed eighty-six degrees Fahrenheit (thirty degrees Celsius) and the growth of the aquatic plants is almost overwhelming. "Every few days we have to remove buckets of *Salvinia auriculata*—a small floating water fern—or it would overtake the pond."

But in winter the pond is appealing, too. Wayne leaves the recirculating pump in place so a continuous stream breaks the surface, preventing some of the water from freezing. The edges of the ice are in constant flux. "Sometimes the area of open water reaches to the edge of the pebbles in the afternoon sun," says Wayne. "Then the house finches, mourning doves and starlings come to bathe and drink. On colder nights, the ice builds up into a dome. Even the dead foliage of the dwarf cattail (*Typha minima*) and the yellow flag iris (*Iris pseudacorus*) look good rising out of ice and making shadows on the snow."

The rest of the garden has also been designed for year-round impact, helped by the sheltered microclimate. One of Wayne's favourites, *Hamamelis* x *intermedia* 'Diane', uncurls its crepe-paper-thin copper petals in the first thaw. "It often opens as early as the second week of February," says Wayne. "And it has fall interest, too—interesting foliage that turns an intense yellow-red." The high stucco walls near the house and the fence help trap the warmth of the early spring sunshine, and in March clumps of nodding white snowdrops (*Galanthus nivalis*) and yellow buttercup-like winter aconites (*Eranthis hyemalis*) peek through the snow. The parade of spring bulbs begins with the lesser-known tulip species *Tulipa tarda* and *T. urumiensis*, and the red *T. linifolia*, which looks striking among the fresh green leaves and blue flowers of periwinkle (*Vinca minor*). Later in May the chequered, nodding heads of *Fritillaria meleagris* appear. Flowering shrubs include eastern redbud (*Cercis canadensis*), another of Wayne's favourite plants. "It's ideal in shape and character for a small garden," he says. "It has subtle pink flowers in spring and good fall colour. I think it's perfect—a nice break from more garish spring flowers."

Below: *Chinese dogwood* (Cornus kousa).

Under the canopy of the redbud grows a Lenten rose (*Helleborus orientalis*). "It's an evergreen, unusual for our climate," Wayne says. "I feel privileged to have it." After the redbud, the Chinese dogwood (*Cornus kousa*) blooms, followed by vines including a large-flowered *Wisteria floribunda* and a climbing hydrangea (*Hydrangea anomala*), which is often called *H. petiolaris*.

"Summer arrives with a wash of yellow," says Wayne. "First we have creeping Jennie

ayne Renaud believes that every well-planned garden should have one strong element that dominates its design. "It's the organizing element," he says, "a measurement or shape you borrow from the house or another structure in the garden, and use as a pattern for the design." In his garden he used the French doors across the front of the coach house, a set of three. The spacing of the doors became a grid pattern, incorporating outer bands. This pattern was used to create a path that leads from the street and past a long, narrow pond to a patio outside the French doors. The path divides the area into a series of well-defined spaces that intrinsically reflect the proportions of the house.

"But it's also important to add interest by breaking up the predictability of the grid system," Wayne says. So he angled the patio edge and slightly skewed the placement of the square fountain set into the pond. The hexagonal windows in the garage/gatehouse and the stucco wall beside the patio are also focal points. "You need a consistent pattern underlying the whole," says Wayne, "but it's the offbeat that gives a garden its dynamic character."

(*Lysimachia nummularia*) along the banks of the pond, and lemon daylilies (*Hemerocallis citrina*) in the perennial bed. Then we have pink astilbes with hostas and ferns dominating the shaded portions of the garden, and white and pale pink impatiens in the periwinkle beds, replacing the spring bulbs."

In summer, the accent is on blue—annual blue lobelia and blue salvia—contrasted with white nicotiana along the pond's edge, which creates a cool mood in the heat of the day.

Fall arrives in the courtyard garden quietly; its sheltered position allows summer to continue well past its usual end. Pink Japanese anemones (*Anemone hupehensis*) begin flowering in early September and continue until early or mid-October. Depending on the weather, they're joined by the fall-flowering crocus (*Crocus sativus*), which has delicate purple petals and saffron yellow stigma, and the false autumn crocus (*Colchicum autumnale*), a double-flowered 'Waterlily' cultivar.

Winter exposes the bones of any garden. Because it's a long season even in southwestern Ontario, Wayne has chosen evergreens to provide the main interest. Two large conifers—an Austrian pine (*Pinus nigra*) and Scots pine (*P. sylvestris*)—provide the major canopy cover. Both were about thirteen feet (four metres) tall when they were planted, so they offered an almost instant effect. *Euonymus kiautschovica* 'Manhattan' and leatherleaf (*Viburnum rhytidophyllum*) also provide winter interest.

The property's clay soil and lack of moisture percolation means the winter water table is very close to the surface. "This limits the things we can plant," says Wayne, "and the pines especially have suffered from the poor drainage." He and Gordon dug the beds to a depth of two feet (sixty centimetres) and heavily amended the soil with sand, composted pine bark and peat moss. The beds are now raised four to ten inches (ten to twenty-five centimetres) above grade.

The walls are made interesting for winter with various forms of English ivies and a semi-evergreen vine *Akebia quinata*. "They all tend to take on shades of deep jade green during winter, and look especially good against the stucco walls and white fences."

Wayne and Gordon spend considerable time in spring and fall planting, pruning and cleaning the pool, but other than that, upkeep is minimal. "The only thing I feel guilty about is allowing the city to take our leaves away," Wayne says, "but we have no space for composting. We do leave some leaves on the beds to rot down, and we mulch them with our own pine needles."

Wayne says he seldom passes through his garden without stopping to enjoy some small thing. "I never cease to marvel at its ability to provide me with a sense of renewal."

Left: *The sun of late summer creates a warm glow in the outdoor living area.*

Far left: *A carpet of leaves marks the changing seasons.*

The Riverside Garden

of Gail & Steve Smith

Photographs by Dudley Witney

he approach to Gail and Steve Smith's garden near St. Stephen, New Brunswick, is enchanting: a country lane winds through a tunnel of dark evergreens and opens suddenly into a sunlit clearing; at the far end of the clearing the garden is revealed, gently tumbling down the rocky hillside to the silvery St. Croix River below. The silky breeze carries the scent of fresh flowers and herbs, enticing the visitor on.

The Smiths found the property while out on their bicycles one warm spring evening more than fourteen years ago. The hillside was a primitive landscape, dotted with rocks and scrubby trees, but they instantly perceived its potential, both as a homestead and a location of beauty. "I saw the hillside as a vacant canvas waiting to be filled with wonderful colours and shapes," says Steve. Today the three-acre (1.2-hectare) property has been transformed into a successful business known as Crocker Hill Studios, with twenty-two display gardens open to the public during the season. Small stone structures exhibit Steve's woodcarvings, paintings and stonework, and Gail's dried herbs and flowers. The rough little cabin that was the only original building was renovated and became the Smiths' home soon after they bought the property.

Above: *One of Steve's beautiful hand-hewn stone benches nestles among bold, cool hosta foliage.*

Curiously, neither Steve nor Gail were much interested in gardening when they stumbled across their future home. As children, both had been assigned the usual garden chores, but serious gardening was alien to them. This soon changed. Their first venture, undertaken in 1980, was a perennial garden on the south side of the cabin. On their bike rides through the surrounding countryside they

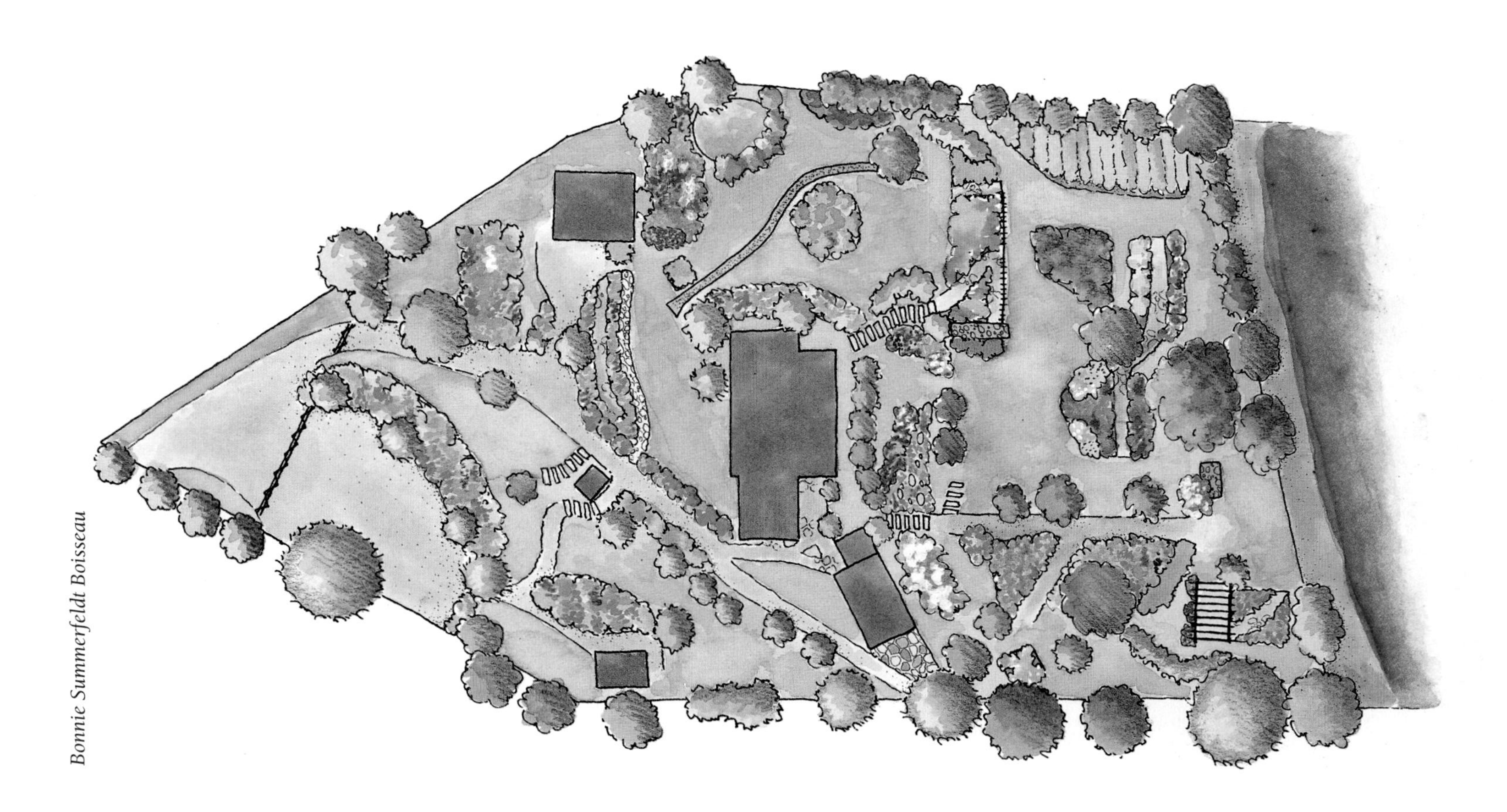

Bonnie Summerfeldt Boisseau

***Previous page:** A view of the garden with the St. Croix River in the background; in the foreground are the purple spikes of statice, with the yellow blooms of oxeye (*Heliopsis helianthoides*), the unopened buds of *Sedum spectabile*, and pink-blooming bergamot (*Monarda didyma*) and phlox.*

noted which homesteads had large clumps of the old-fashioned perennials they like so much; later they asked the owners for a root division. Over the years the border evolved into a valuable collection of old favourites—Oriental poppies (*Papaver orientale*), several cultivars of peonies, and the old, red form of sweet bergamot (*Monarda didyma*), among others.

Another project—the stand of lupins in their lawn area—wasn't so successful. "They looked beautiful on the roadsides, great swaths of colour," says Gail. "But we learned pretty quickly that they attract aphids. So they all went, except for one plant in the perennial bed."

Developing the hillside was a major task. "Our address is Ledge Road," says Steve ruefully, "and we soon found out how it got its name. One part of the hill was dry and gravelly, so we rebuilt it with peat and compost, and then mulched heavily to retain moisture. Even then, soil kept washing away, so we built a system of locks to prevent heavy rains from gushing down the driveway."

The French drain that carries excess water away from the garden is more than utilitarian: it's also an attractive focal point, lined with smooth grey pebbles and edged with moss- and lichen-covered rocks hand picked by Steve. It meanders gently through the lawn, following the curve of the flower border. The dike system beside the driveway is built of blocks of red and grey granite from an unused quarry nearby. Each piece was chosen carefully by Steve, who admits he spent hours selecting and cutting just the right ones. The rocks also lend their beauty to Steve's handmade benches and retaining walls, and the exquisite stone pathways that lead visitors through the garden.

Like all gardens, the Smiths' is continually expanding. "When you start a garden you have to visualize how it will look three years ahead," says Steve. "Otherwise you'd plant too many trees too close together, and have flower beds so densely packed the plants would yellow and grow poorly for lack of space."

Below: *Virginia creeper completely clothes the garden shed; black-eyed Susan (*Rudbeckia hirta*) adds a splash of colour in the foreground.*

You also have to maintain healthy soil. Steve and Gail compost all their leaves after putting them through their new shredder. "It was a great investment," says Steve. "We shred leaves and plant debris so they break down faster, and we do this at any time of the year— even in winter, when a place where the snow has melted might reveal leaves." They also add cattle manure and seaweed to the soil. "And we always have manure tea steeping for our plants."

The extensive herb gardens were inspired by a book on herbs Gail received as a Christmas gift in 1981. At first, the couple grew them to add interest to their vegetarian diet, but soon they were planning themed herb gardens. Luckily there was a good nursery close by with a wide selection of herbs, and more recent trips to a nursery in Camden, Maine, has augmented the collection, despite the inconvenience of having to have plants inspected by federal agricultural authorities before they can be brought across the border. The Smiths' present herb collection is one of the largest in eastern Canada and their gardens have many themes, including a medicinal garden, featuring many traditional and modern plants. In the tea garden, they grow herbs

teve Smith loves rocks, and he's collected dozens from an abandoned quarry near his home to give his sloping garden a theme. Not only does he have a keen eye for handsome rocks, he seems to know just where to place them for best effect.

In the Smiths' New Brunswick garden, rock walls and paths create a continuous thread, leading from one intriguing theme garden to the next.

Square rocks provide steps of just the right height and width—an important consideration in a garden that's open to the public, which the Smiths' is. Steve's stone benches are carefully placed seats where one can drink in the scents and colours of the garden. Benches are often a bit of a joke to gardeners because they never sit on them: if they do, it's just long enough to notice an area which needs weeding. But for the visitor, comfortable seating is important. The stone Steve uses is a warm grey, which blends well with the thyme that fill the gaps between stepping-stones in the pathways. As visitors walk over it, the air is filled with its herb-scented aroma. Another good plant for this purpose is Corsican mint (*Mentha requinii*); its scent is strong enough to fill the whole garden when it is bruised.

Rocks may seem a bit cumbersome for small urban gardens, but if they're carefully placed they can add much interest. For example, one massive rock at the end of a curved path in a bed of river pebbles can create a destination.

like chamomile, anise hyssop and pineapple sage (it isn't hardy in their area and has to be treated as an annual or wintered over in the tiny unheated greenhouse). "Many of the mints make wonderful teas," says Gail, "but the plants are invasive and tend to take over the garden. So every spring Steve lifts and divides them all." The mint collection includes spearmint, pineapple mint, orange mint and their favourite, apple mint.

The fragrant garden is particularly popular with visitors. One is welcomed to it by a large southernwood (*Artemisia abrotanum*) whose aromatic foliage fills the air as you brush past it. Several old-fashioned sweet-smelling roses are underplanted with dwarf catmint; clumps of spicy dianthus are dotted about; and pennyroyal, lemon thyme and orange balsam thyme appear here and there. Of course, there is lavender. What would a fragrant garden be without lavender?

Above: *A fine arbour provides a cool seating area overlooking a modern knot garden.*

The silver garden is delightful, with lavender and lamb's ears forming dense, silvery patches with santolina. Santolina is borderline hardy in New Brunswick, as is another of Gail's favourites, Russian sage (*Perovskia atriplicifolia* 'Blue Spire'). "Sometimes we lose them, especially if there isn't enough snow cover," she says. "But one or two plants always survive." Other gardens that delight visitors include the edible blossom garden, the onion and chive garden, and the vegetable garden.

Clearly, herbs are the Smiths' plants of choice. "They fit well with our natural landscape," says Steve. "Every one has its own beauty. We have creeping thyme that comes up grey-green under the apple tree in spring and later becomes a thick green mat that one feels compelled to walk barefoot through. We particularly like the green-blue rue (*Ruta graveolens*)—but so does the parsley worm, which devours the foliage. We also enjoy the sweet woodruff (*Galium oderatum*) that comes up in spring underneath the cedar trees."

Even comfrey (*Symphytum officinale*) has its place in the Smiths' garden. "We filled a damp area with it," says Steve. "And even if we don't use it for anything else, its leaves make great compost."

The Smiths are dedicated organic gardeners and never use chemical sprays. They invested in ladybugs, which settled well into the environment and control some pests, and have several resident toads that feast on others. They're constantly on the watch for infestations of eggs, which are hand picked and destroyed as soon as they appear. Should a pest escape their notice and become established, they concoct garlic and other herb-based sprays with soap to eradicate the problem.

"Gardening means working with nature," says Steve. "To me, it's another form of art, an extension of my studio. I love creating attractive spaces, or searching for just the right stone to complete a current project. But all the while, in my mind I'm visualizing the next one."

Left: *An artistically designed French drain combines the practical and the beautiful in Steve and Gail's garden.*

Right: *Purple cone flower* (Echinacea purpurea), *globe thistle* (Echinops ritro), *marigolds* (Tagetes *'Golden Gem'*), *and assorted herbs create a border of texture, colour and scent.*

The Prairie Garden

of Jeanine Smith

Photographs by Michael Brauer

If one was dropped from a helicopter blindfolded into Jeanine Smith's glorious garden in the middle of July, one might not guess its location was Saskatoon, Saskatchewan. The mere mention of this city conjures up mental pictures of frozen winters and hot, dry summers, but in fact it's a gem, with friendly tree-lined streets and a tranquil park that follows the curve of the South Saskatchewan River. And Jeanine Smith's garden, although modest in size, sparkles in its midst.

Phil and Jeanine's small grey-green house on a corner lot is typical of the Prairies. It's squarish and unassuming, with a vegetable garden running parallel to the lane at the back, and pretty foundation plantings at the front. What you notice as you walk down the path from the street is how the plants match the house in a pleasing monochromatic scheme: hanging baskets overflow with white flowers and grey-green foliage plants; shrubs include soft green cedars and junipers interplanted with variegated dogwood (*Cornus sericea alba*). To the right of the entrance, dogwood curves gracefully around the northwest corner of the house; a brick path leads to the left, and the entrance to the rear garden. Along the way, in a shady home at the corner of the house, all kinds of woodland plants thrive: *Primula veris* and *P. saxatilis*; pulmonarias, including the species *Pulmonaria longifolia* and the cultivars 'Sissinghurst White', 'Bowles Red', and 'Janet Fisk' (Jeanine's favourite because of its bold silver leaves). Several species of hostas with blue, green and yellow variegated leaves also grow here. One is subliminally aware of a careful balance of colour and texture, but it isn't until one rounds the back

Above: *A fine water feature can be created with something as simple as a half-barrel.*

Bonnie Summerfeldt Boisseau

Previous page: *The drumstick flowers of pale mauve alliums, yellow lilies (*Lilium hybridum*), and yarrow (*Achillea millefolium*) complement each other in this mixed border.*

corner of the house and catches sight of the English-style perennial border that Jeanine's colour artistry becomes abundantly obvious.

The perennial border is viewed from the brick patio in the L of the house. It has built-in benches, an archway that runs from the shed to the house and frames the view, and a still pond in a half barrel, in which grows a clump of miniature cattail (*Typha minima*). Up the house scrambles a grape; over the shed and the arch clematis, Virginia creeper and honeysuckle happily cohabit. The vines were carefully selected for seasonal interest: the clematis 'Bluebird' is hardy in the shelter of the house and blooms in early spring with the 'Dropmore Scarlet' honeysuckle; the fluffy seed pods of the clematis also provide winter interest. In fall, Virginia creeper (*Parthenocissus quinquefolia*) brightens the area with splashes of red and orange leaves.

The scene framed by the arch is reminiscent of an English garden. The perennial border is a tapestry of colour, balanced by the grey-green of several varieties of artemisia and backed by the green of a clipped cotoneaster hedge. Jeanine loves yellows, and a recent favourite is a perennial evening primrose (*Oenothera fruticosa*) in clear, bright yellow, which she places near a drift of pale yellow 'Dawn Star' lilies. A feature of the purple, pink and mauve area is *Filipendula rubra*, a prairie native that blooms profusely with fluffy rose-pink flowers. Among the artemisias are 'Lambrook Silver', 'Silver Mound', and 'Silver Brocade', a recent introduction from the University of British Columbia.

Many varieties Jeanine likes aren't readily available at local garden centres, so she grows most of her plants from seed. She says being a member of the Devonian Botanic Garden at the University of Alberta in Edmonton gives her access to their seed list, which is a good source of hardy varieties, and at the back of her garden she runs her own little test plot. She leaves the seedlings in the plot until they bloom so she can assess their colour and growth habit. Then she decides where they should go in her garden. "But my colour planning is mainly trial and error," she says. "My favourites change frequently. I may prefer one of the new plants until it's been around for a few seasons; then it seems commonplace and another, newer one takes its place." She advises gardeners who forget what their beds and borders look like to keep written records and also to take snapshots several times a season.

Above: *A pleasing scene framed by the silvery foliage of a Russian olive* (Elaeagnus angustifolia).

On the south side of the house is a rock garden with all kinds of dianthus, including *Dianthus* x *allwoodii* 'Alpinus', a sweetly scented variety that comes in deep rose through pale pink and white; and *D. gratianopolitanus*, cheddar pink, an old English cottage-garden variety with many tiny deep-rose to carmine flowers forming vivid cushions of colour. From the rock garden one's eye is drawn to a good-sized ash tree that divides the back garden from the front. Under the ash and into the shrub border on the street side grows a patch of bold, shiny-leaved bergenia. The shrub border, too, is carefully colour coordinated: *Potentilla fruticosa*, which has bright golden flowers all summer long; variegated red osier dogwoods *Cornus sericea* 'Aurea'; a soft mound of *Pinus*

eanine Smith's desire for unusual perennials led her to join the Devonian Botanic Garden at the University of Alberta. She has grown many of the perennials offered in their seed list. This involves not only patience, since many don't bloom for two to three years, but tender loving care. Perennial seeds should be sown inside in early March, and some require a cold treatment beforehand.

Store them in damp peat moss in a plastic bag in the fridge for four to six weeks. Sow seeds in sterilized potting soil and keep them dark, warm and moist until they germinate. After sprouting put them under lights for fourteen hours a day in a cool basement. Maintain a temperature of fifty to fifty-four degrees Fahrenheit (ten to twelve degrees Celsius) by day and forty-six degrees Fahrenheit (eight degrees Celsius) at night. Air circulation is also important.

Transplant seedlings into individual four-inch (ten-centimetre) pots when they're large enough to handle, and move to a cold frame outside as soon as the weather begins to warm up. Generally this is from early April through May. In late May seedlings can be planted out into a row in the vegetable garden or, as Jeanine does, in a test plot. Because water is often scarce on the Prairies, she mulches them with grass clippings. Their growth, height and colour is recorded, and when they are large enough they are transferred to the perennial border.

mugo looking like a big green hedgehog; and *Spiraea* x *bumaldi* 'Goldflame', which sports a good bronze colour on the new growth in spring. Under a Russian olive (*Elaeagnus angustifolia*), a feature of the garden, with narrow silver-backed leaves that ripple in the prairie breeze, a dense groundcover of bright yellow creeping Jennie (*Lysimachia nummelaria*) looks like a pool reflecting the golden variegation of the nearby dogwoods. A hedge of deciduous highbush cranberries (*Viburnum opulus*) and a pretty wooden arbour (like the patio and arch, they were made by Phil Smith) divide the ornamental garden from the vegetable patch and the working area at the rear. Next to the trial border is a large compost bin, easily accessible from the brick path. Raspberries and asparagus are easy to reach for harvesting and weeding, as is the two-tiered herb bed, constructed from railroad ties. Spikes of bluish-violet hyssop (*Hyssopus officinalis*) and bluish-silver catnip (*Nepeta cataria*) are a cool note complemented by brilliant carnation-flowered annual poppies (*Papaver somniferum*); running amok through all of this are the chartreuse umbels of dillweed (*Anethum graveolens*).

The rest of the back section is devoted to vegetables set in soldierly rows: several kinds of tomatoes (such as the early-ripening 'Early Girl' and 'Pixie', which produces lots of cherry-type fruit with old-fashioned tomato flavour); corn (Jeanine's favourite is 'Northern Supersweet'); carrots ('Ingot', a short-season variety, has good flavour and keeping qualities); and beets (the cylindrical varieties, because they cook quickly and evenly).

The Smiths' soil is a heavy clay, so composting is important. The beds are frequently top-dressed, and well-rotted manure is dug in. Sand is also used as an amendment. "I know lots of garden books say never to add sand to clay soil because it compacts it," says Jeanine. "But I find it helps ours. It stays in the soil for years—long after the compost and manure have been absorbed."

***Left:** A shady path at the side of Jeanine's house makes a perfect home for daylilies* (Hemerocallis fulva)*, hardy catmint* (Nepeta sibirica)*, and variegated plants.*

***Far left:** Jeanine's tapestry of perennials, many of which were grown from seed.*

69

The Old-Fashioned Garden

of Nancy & Ted Maitland
Photographs by Christopher Dew

Ted and Nancy Maitland's friends might have been forgiven for wondering why the couple would even consider buying such a ramshackle house. They might have agreed the 140-year-old stone structure had possibilities: it's a small but graceful home typical of the type around Kitchener, Ontario, where they live, but it had been empty for six years and was suffering from neglect. In addition, there was a skeleton of a burned-out barn in the back yard. "The front yard was so out of control, just trying to mow the grass was a major chore," says Ted. "And the back was a wasteland of burned timbers, twisted metal and barbed wire."

Above: *The purple blooms of chives set off the delicate pink of an old-fashioned rose.*

But that was 1982. In the intervening years both house and garden have undergone a miraculous transformation, and today just passing it is like taking a step back in time. Restoration of the house was, of course, the first priority. "But the garden was important too," says Ted. "We conceived it initially as part of our restoration project, researching plants of the mid-1800s. But our interest in gardening overtook our desire for historical accuracy." They soon abandoned the restrictions they'd imposed on themselves and concentrated on maintaining the look of an old-fashioned garden.

Soon after they bought the house, on one-third of an acre (.13-hectare), the wheatfield behind it was sold for a new subdivision. "During construction the road became incredibly busy, so the first year we planted a privet hedge for privacy," says Ted. It's now well established. The next project was a rose arbour to welcome visitors and define the front entrance.

The first fall they also planted a mass of daffodil bulbs, and planned a

Bonnie Summerfeldt Boisseau

Previous page: *Irises and lupins dominate the front garden.*

dooryard garden of symmetrically placed square beds and grass paths on either side of a central walkway. Over the years, the dooryard garden has been enlarged to take up most of the front yard, and the grass paths have been replaced by flagstones. "The stone eliminates mowing and edging and gives us more room for plants," says Ted. "It also means the garden is less dewy in the early morning, so it's more accessible for inspections." A bench, sundial and bird bath have been added as focal points for both summer and winter, but it's the profusion of flowers that makes the front garden. "We have a sort of agreement that the front is his and the back is mine," says Nancy with a smile. "But to be honest, Ted does the hard work in both."

Ted's favourite inhabitants of the front garden are the roses. "Particularly the David Austin roses," he says, "and I like three the best—'Yeoman', 'Lilian Austin', and 'The Squire'. But I am a little disappointed at how slow they are to get going, compared to other old-fashioned roses, like 'Soleil'. It has a multitude of blooms each summer. I also like lupins, some of which I grow from seed. But a couple of winters back we didn't get sufficient snow cover and I lost quite a few." Bearded iris (*Iris germanica*) also grow in the front garden, a clear yellow form and a blue, and the hardy geranium 'Johnson's Blue'. Ted is proud of the flagstone path, and particularly likes the thymes that grow in the cracks, softening the hard edges of the stone and adding to the fragrance in the air.

The back garden was more of a challenge, partly because the contractor in charge of the house renovation buried the cobblestones and other debris removed from an old porch in its earth. "The first year, all we did was put in some grass beside the house," says Nancy. "The next spring we planted raspberry canes and a few vegetables in raised beds, using lumber from the old outbuildings." That spring they also discovered that brisk westerly winds swept across the back yard, so Ted dug up the year-old grass he'd planted so carefully and piled the sod to create a windbreak. "Of course, he really wanted to put garden beds where the grass was," laughs Nancy. Winter frosts had dislodged the buried cobblestones and some from the foundation of the old barn, and these were used to start a garden wall. "But we later moved the wall," Nancy says. "We improved it and enlarged it almost annually, as we worked on the back garden, reclaiming more of the land every year."

Below: *Nancy's back garden with her newly established herb gardens in the background.*

There was an old lilac hedge at the east side of the property, and the Maitlands retained as much as possible for privacy between their house and the new subdivision. Ted planted more quick-growing privet on the south and west sides of the lot, and a tall hedge of shrubby honeysuckle attracts birds and shields the north side.

Nancy's garden at the back is more formal than her husband's, but she shares his love of roses. Arbours are covered with the old-fashioned white 'Prosperity' and the sweetbriar 'Lucy Bertrams', which sends the delightful scent of its foliage and flowers over the garden in June. Nancy also has a soft spot for herbs of all kinds, so the back contains a formal herb garden with gravel pathways and a central sundial. "I try different herbs each year, depending on whether I want them for the kitchen or for dried flowers," says Nancy. "But I always grow basil. It does so well here and it makes good pesto. I also like mints, for drying and winter use, particularly ginger mint. And clary sage, which reseeds itself faithfully year after year." Last

Nancy and Ted Maitland like to start annuals indoors, but they prefer to use their own compost as a medium rather than using a store-bought mix. To be sure it's disease and weed free they sterilize several batches each fall, then keep it bagged for spring. The moist, screened compost is placed in a sealed roasting bag with a meat thermometer stuck in it and baked in an oven preheated to 325 degrees Fahrenheit (162 degrees Celsius). Once the compost has reached 180 degrees Fahrenheit (82 degrees Celsius), it's removed from the oven and spread on a clean surface to cool quickly before it's bagged and stored.

A covered roasting pan can also be used. However, sterilizing soil or compost in the oven can leave an objectionable smell wafting through the house. You could follow the example of a Calgary gardener who does his on the gas barbecue, or the practice of Stan Hutrya, who gardens in Yellowknife in the Northwest Territories. He sterilizes a large amount of soil in an old metal drum with holes drilled at two-inch (five-centimetre) intervals in the bottom. He places the drum over an outdoor fire or barbecue pit and lights the coals.

year she discovered the small English daisy *Bellis perennis* and it's become a favourite.

The herb garden evolved from Nancy's interest in cooking, and she started with a small culinary herb bed. "We found some nice old bricks at a dump, and made paths. All of a sudden, garden design became as much fun as gardening. The paths were changed frequently—the bricks are still there, now as edging, but now we have gravel paths separating the beds." When she developed an interest in dried flowers, the herb garden had to be enlarged again; then some research on old roses resulted in the need for space. "Vegetables have been reduced to squash plants on top of the compost pile and the odd self-seeding rogue tomato plant," says Nancy.

A large and handsome latticed pergola in the back garden provides support for roses and wisteria, and shade for a bed next to the rectangular pond. The pond was inspired by a visit to another garden. "Water gardening seemed so easy, and it looked so beautiful," says Nancy. "So we redesigned the herb garden to make room for a pond. Then came the pergola, and it's been great—it gives us some shade, which we didn't have before, and allowed us to put in hostas, lamium and a rhododendron."

They also planned a service area, which too few gardeners allow space for. "We call it the administrative area," says Nancy. "It's in a back corner, hidden from the house by privet hedge, and it contains three compost heaps and two garden sheds. Closer to the house we have two prefabricated composters for kitchen waste, and we keep them all on the go. In fall we screen bags of stuff from the cold compost heaps and bake it, then use it in spring to start seeds."

Like most gardens, the Maitlands' has evolved as time and budget allow. And they do have places to relax in their garden—a string hammock is hung every year under the pergola, and a classic garden bench sits nearby. But they're barely used. "We'll sit down now and then," says Nancy, "but after a few minutes' rest one or both of us is up weeding or dead-heading again."

Left: *The old-fashioned briar rose 'Lucy Bertrams' covers the arbour.*

Far Left: *Unopened buds of lavender* (Lavandula angustifolia), *perennial geranium* (Geranium himalayense), *snow-in-summer* (Cerastium tomentosum), *bearded iris* (Iris germanica) *and other perennials form a lush planting around the pathway.*

The Classic Garden

of Doris Fancourt-Smith

Photographs by Paddy Wales

oris and Peter Fancourt-Smith's Vancouver garden was inspired by their new deck, a wide, handsome structure that wraps around two sides of the grey stucco house and reflects its classic lines. "When we put the deck on in 1988, I suddenly realized how much I loved symmetry," says Doris. "I admired its formal structure, its circle-and-square motif, and the way it tied into the design of the house. I decided to adopt some of these ideas in the new garden."

Doris and Peter had been planning to renovate their garden for years. The children were grown, and the corner lot, always perfect for a family with its large swath of lawn for soccer games and plenty of trees for climbing, seemed in need of a more adult approach. The first step was to construct the deck, which did more than awaken Doris's appreciation for geometric shapes and formal design—it revealed a series of mini-views from the house. From the dining room's French doors, for example, Doris found that her eye was drawn down the deck steps to the back lawn; here she created a focal point by planting a circle of lady's mantle (*Alchemilla mollis*) and centring it with a bird bath. In the side yard, down another set of steps outside the study, Doris and Peter installed a small reflecting pool, which Doris finds a source of inspiration when she's working. (With four other Master Gardeners, Doris helped write *The Twelve Month Gardener*, a book for west-coasters.)

Above: *A traditional clipped boxwood hedge* (Buxus microphylla) *outlines a bed of herbs.*

The garden, in fact, is a series of intimate areas, or garden rooms. Once past the tall hedge of mixed evergreens that encloses the property, one finds oneself in a large, formal entrance garden looking at the inviting,

Previous page: *Peter Fancourt-Smith's magnificent gazebo is clothed with vines carefully selected by Doris.*

silver-grey house through the branches of a gorgeous, plum-coloured Japanese maple. To the right of the front steps lies a four-square, medieval-style garden, each square centred with a star magnolia (*Magnolia stellata*). In spring, the magnolias are covered with creamy blooms; in winter their silver-grey, furry buds seem to glow during Vancouver's dreary weather. In any season the trees are visible from the living room, set against the deep green hedge.

Past the entrance planting, a tall lattice fence and arch beckon you into another area. This one echoes the curve of the deck with a circle of grass edged with hydrangeas. Below the balustrade grows snow-in-summer (*Cerastium tomentosum*), its strong silver foliage picking up the colour of the house. Above it, on the balustrade, old-fashioned pink climbing roses intertwine with the gorgeous, violet-purple flowers of *Clematis jackmanii*.

Across the circle of grass grow the hydrangeas (*Hydrangea macrophylla*), a curved border of stunning deep blue underplanted with lime-green lady's mantle (*Alchemilla mollis*). Behind them, peeking out from under the hedge, is a mixed border of low-growing perennials, including bright spring-blooming primulas. Setting off the scene is a large clump of white hydrangeas (*Hydrangea arborescens*) and another dark red Japanese maple.

The Fancourt-Smiths' lawns are typical of the west coast, containing a good measure of bright green moss and clover as well as grass. "In the new garden, the lawns are background," Doris says. "Their lovely green texture complements the beds and borders. And we welcome moss and weeds—they add interest. Trying to keep a lawn moss-free on the west coast takes too much work." Doris and Peter aerate the lawns each spring, before top-dressing with lime and sand. But they never use fertilizer, and they don't irrigate the lawns, even in dry spells.

Above: *Blue* Hydrangea macrophylla *and pure white* Hydrangea arborescens *invite entry into this cool green room.*

The next tiny room lies up a couple of shallow old-brick steps. This garden is paved and home to the formal, rectangular pool. Beyond it, a welcoming white bench encourages one to linger a while. The pool once contained water lilies and fish, but they lost an ongoing battle with the raccoons. Now it's a plantless, fishless, serene sheet of black water that mirrors a tall native dogwood (*Cornus nuttallii*). This area is a study in formal balance: borders planted with several hosta species and frothy green lady's mantle (*Alchemilla mollis*) edge the pool and are framed by exposed aggregate paving. Lady's mantle is particularly attractive in a west coast garden because its leaves catch the raindrops and hold them around the serrated edges like diamonds.

Of course, it wasn't just the deck that inspired Doris's garden design. Over the years she's honed her interest in gardening with many books, including Russell Page's *The Education of a Gardener*. "It was the biggest influence," she says. On their travels, she and Peter have visited many public and private gardens. "In those gardens I found I was attracted to garden rooms and intimate spaces. I think it may have something to do with my mother's and grandmother's gardens in Ireland. I grew up in enclosed

he handsome gazebo and other structures in Doris Fancourt-Smith's garden were designed as part of the overall plan to form a series of rooms. Each has an arch or gateway that beckons the visitor to move through it and on to the next garden room. Each also supports some kind of vine or climber. Doris points out that the structures give interest and height to an otherwise flat garden and successfully tie the design together. The large, custom-designed gazebo was based on one in a Scottish garden; Doris saw a picture in a magazine and kept it on her fridge for inspiration. Other structures were inspired by those seen in books borrowed from the library.

When the time came to build the structures for their new garden, Doris came up with the drawings and her husband, Peter, worked on the plans. His experience as a hobby woodworker was an invaluable asset. The gazebo, perhaps the centrepiece of the garden, is about twenty feet (six metres) square and sixteen feet (five metres) high at its tallest point, large enough for grass paths through it and vines and perennials around the base on all four corners. They used pressure-treated lumber set in concrete, and painted the gazebo white to tie in with the other structures in the garden.

gardens, and they feel comfortable to me." Vita Sackville-West's famous garden at Sissinghurst Castle in England impressed Doris most. "I was fascinated by the way an archway would pull your eye and draw you into the next garden."

From the pool garden, a path leads to the rear garden and the gazebo, a square lattice structure built by Peter at the end of a grassy path lined with perennials, a rhododendron and a barberry (*Berberis vulgaris*), two of the garden's original shrubs. Peter loves to build, so Doris happily searched

out designs from magazines and garden books, drew up some plans, and handed them over to him. He did a superb job on all the structures, but the gazebo is his triumph. Now, five years after the garden was begun, it tumbles with roses and *Clematis montana*. The four beds at the corners are bursting with irises, hardy geraniums and a purple smoke tree (*Cotinus coggygria*); its rich, plum-coloured foliage is kept pruned tightly back so there is always plenty of strong growth. Tucked under the house on the other side of the grass path is a border of pale pink polyantha roses 'The Fairy', which bloom all summer and are mildew resistant, making them perfect for the damp climate. Showing them off to perfection is an underplanting of lamb's ears (*Stachys byzantina*).

Directly behind the house is the big view—an expanse of lawn with a curved planting of *Photinia fraserii* at the far end. A large native cedar (*Thuja plicata*), in which the children used to play, has been limbed to provide more light and space for the lawn, and it's balanced by a pink-flowered eastern native dogwood (*Cornus florida*).

Another bit of Peter's handiwork, a classic arbour with a graceful arch, runs nearly the length of the lawn, dividing it from a formal medieval garden that opens off the kitchen. A perennial border filled with ornamental grasses, peonies, phlox, dianthus, and hardy geraniums forms a tapestry of textures at the base of the arbour. In midsummer the border is backed by a hundred 'Casa Blanca' lilies that perfume the whole garden.

Above: *Hostas and* Alchemilla mollis *soften the edge of the reflecting pool.*

Left: *Careful placement of plants and structures complete this room in Doris's garden.*

The circle-in-a-cross medieval garden has a floor of old mossy bricks centred with a stone sundial. Each of the four beds is edged with boxwood, which sets off the centre plantings of lavender (*Lavandula angustifolia* 'Munstead'), 'Iceberg' roses, and white lavatera. A colour scheme of white, pink and blue flowers set off by silver foliage predominates in the garden at present, but gardens tend to evolve with the gardener's taste. In earlier years Doris favoured hot colours—scarlet salvia and yellow marigolds—and she admits she's probably entering a white phase now.

Behind the garage is the compost and work area. Every spring Doris top-dresses the beds with a layer of compost and mushroom manure she gets from a local grower. The garden is a lot of hard work, she admits, but it also provides the couple with much pleasure. "I probably do my best thinking in it," she says.

Further Reading

Bennett, Jennifer, and Turid Forsyth. *The Harrowsmith Annual Garden*. Camden East: Camden House, 1990.

Brickell, Christopher and Trevor Cole. *Practical Guide to Gardening in Canada*. Montreal: Reader's Digest, 1993.

Chatto, Beth. *The Green Tapestry*. New York: Simon and Schuster, 1989.

Cole, Trevor. *The Ontario Gardener*. Vancouver: Whitecap Books, 1991.

Damrosch, Barbara. *The Garden Primer*. New York: Workman, 1988.

Gardner, Jo Ann. *The Heirloom Garden*. Pownall, Vermont: Storey Communications, 1992.

Harris, Marjorie. *The Canadian Gardener's Guide to Foliage and Garden Design*. Toronto: Random House, 1993.

Hobhouse, Penelope. *Color in Your Garden*. Boston: Little, Brown and Company, 1984.

———. *Garden Style*. Boston: Little, Brown and Company, 1988.

Hole, Lois. *Northern Flower Gardening*. Edmonton: Lone Pine, 1994.

Keeble, Midge Ellis. *Tottering in My Garden*. Camden East: Camden House, 1989.

Kennedy, Des. *Crazy About Gardening*. Vancouver: Whitecap Books, 1994.

Lima, Patrick. *The Harrowsmith Perennial Garden*. Camden East: Camden House, 1987.

Lovejoy, Ann. *The Year in Bloom*. Seattle: Sasquatch Books, 1989.

Osborne, Robert. *Roses for Canadian Gardens*. Toronto: Key Porter, 1991.

Toop, Edgar W. *Annuals for the Prairies*. Edmonton: University of Alberta Faculty of Extension, 1993.

Toop, Edgar W. and Sara Williams. *Perennials for the Prairies*. Edmonton: University of Alberta Faculty of Extension, 1991.

Verey, Rosemary. *The Scented Garden*. New York: Random House, 1981.

Vick, Roger. *Gardening on the Prairies*. Saskatoon: Western Producer Prairie Books, 1987.

INDEX